December 2016

A MOST IMPROBABLE ADVENTURE

To John & Kim,

A month or so ago, this book was delivered to me — well, a copy of this one. This was written by Colin's brother, Jason, and inside was a personalized note to me — about the influence Earl had on him and on Colin. It took me completely by surprise as I had no idea this book was being written OR that Earl had been such an impact. I promised I'd buy a copy for you for Christmas — as I think all the people Earl held so dearly in his life should have one — so I'll start with the ones I know! Love, Jane

A MOST IMPROBABLE ADVENTURE

OVERLAND FROM MEXICO CITY TO PANAMA CITY

JASON THIESSEN

iUniverse®

A MOST IMPROBABLE ADVENTURE
OVERLAND FROM MEXICO CITY TO PANAMA CITY

Copyright © 2016 Jason Thiessen.
Cover photo by Jason Thiessen.

All rights reserved. No part of this book may be used or reproduced by any means, graphic, electronic, or mechanical, including photocopying, recording, taping or by any information storage retrieval system without the written permission of the author except in the case of brief quotations embodied in critical articles and reviews.

iUniverse books may be ordered through booksellers or by contacting:

iUniverse
1663 Liberty Drive
Bloomington, IN 47403
www.iuniverse.com
1-800-Authors (1-800-288-4677)

Because of the dynamic nature of the Internet, any web addresses or links contained in this book may have changed since publication and may no longer be valid. The views expressed in this work are solely those of the author and do not necessarily reflect the views of the publisher, and the publisher hereby disclaims any responsibility for them.

Any people depicted in stock imagery provided by Thinkstock are models, and such images are being used for illustrative purposes only. Certain stock imagery © Thinkstock.

ISBN: 978-1-4917-9141-7 (sc)
ISBN: 978-1-4917-9140-0 (e)

Library of Congress Control Number: 2016906728

Print information available on the last page.

iUniverse rev. date: 05/16/2016

Other books by Jason Thiessen:

Around My World: A Detour on Life's Journey

CONTENTS

Dedication ix
Acknowledgements..xi

What's wrong with you? 1
Voices departed 7
The museum is closed 21
The Forester and the Filmmaker......................... 45
El Fuego awakens 83
Memory and truth 115
The Dane and the Kiwi 129
Just don't kill me 185
Leaving America... 205

DEDICATION

To Colin – thank you for being my big brother, my role model, and my friend.

To Earl – thank you for your lifetime of friendship to Colin. You are deeply missed.

ACKNOWLEDGEMENTS

My wife Isabelle has been by my side for over seventeen years and of her many, many demonstrations of love for me her support of the journey upon which this book is based is perhaps the greatest. At a time of change and difficulty in our lives she did not panic or wilt like a flower in the hot sun. She asked herself, "What makes my husband happy?" She didn't withdraw and hide nor did she point out the obvious challenges. She thought not of herself, but of me. "What makes my husband happy?" led to the obvious answer: travel.

Sam and Will, our two amazing boys, were three-and-a-half and eight months old at the time. She was a full-time mom and part-time entrepreneur. Her husband was a 41-year-old recently unemployed and slightly damaged man. "What makes my husband happy?" superceeded all of the myriad other questions in her mind. Now that's love.

I had been thinking about what to do with my time since my layoff, other than trying to find another soul-sucking job, that is. It crossed my mind that I should travel while I had the chance. I struggled with the thought as I considered the implications. My family needed me to work, not to travel; or so I thought. Isabelle knew what I was thinking, I didn't have to say anything. One night after we had put the boys to bed the subject came up – and she had an idea. She said I should use the time to go traveling. My rather sudden freedom was a gift after all. She said all I needed to do was decide where and for how long. There was no debate, no argument, no guilt, and no convincing required. She knew what made me happy – and it still does. Sweetie, thank you for all that you are and for bringing out the best in me.

I also want to acknowledge my brother-in-law, Isabelle's brother Pierre-Luc. During the writing of this book he was struck with cancer. At the age of thirty-four he was shocked to discover that he had a rare form of Hodgkin's disease. This was a blow to the family, and it hit me hard. I could not imagine how such a young, physically strong man could have this poison in his body. It simply was not fair. Not long before his diagnosis he had received the happiest news of his life – he was going to be a dad. I couldn't even imagine what he must have been thinking. He was a newlywed, about to become a father, and was given perhaps the worst news possible.

After the devastating news Isabelle jumped into big sister mode. She was on the phone nearly every day speaking with him, letting him express what he was going through. She would talk to me about their conversations. She spoke of his acceptance of the situation, of his desire to work through it as a matter of course. I spoke with him once early on and told him how I thought his approach was the best way to handle it. I told him this was simply an obstacle, a detour in his life, it would not be what defined him. Every time I saw him afterward, which was not as often as I would have liked due to the distance between where we lived, I shook his hand and pulled him in for a hug, a long hug. I wanted to squeeze the cancer out.

For the next several months Pierre-Luc went through chemotherapy treatments, then radiation therapy. He did everything he was *supposed* to do. But he went further. He went inside and asked himself some hard questions. He got in touch with his spirit. We met for coffee at one point and I almost couldn't believe what I witnessed. I sat in front of a very ill man who had accepted his circumstance but had not accepted his fate. He was living *with* the cancer, going inside and politely asking it to leave. He wasn't *fighting* anything, for fighting ensured he would have an emboldened opponent – one that he simply did not want to stand toe-to-toe with. He knew the cancer was there to send him a message and now it was time for the cancer to go. I had never seen someone so at peace in my life. I teared up as I listened to him talk. I was so moved. He reminded me, without saying it, what was important in life.

Prior to the completion of this book he received what must have truly been music to his ears: "You are all clear." When Isabelle told me the news I nearly wept. I was so relieved and so very, very happy for him. He would have many, many years to be a husband and a father to his beautiful baby boy.

We've all had difficult times in our lives, but not all of us have handled it with love, gratitude, and grace; you've done exactly that, Pierre-Luc. Thank you for showing me, and all of us, the way.

WHAT'S WRONG WITH YOU?

The conversation between me, an unemployed 41-year-old husband and father of two young boys, and a composite of nearly everyone I spoke to about my going on a solo overland trip from Mexico City to Panama City, sounded something like this:

"What the hell are you thinking?"

"What do you mean?"

"You have a three-year-old and an eight-month-old at home, you have no job, and your wife is trying to raise kids and run a business at the same time!"

"Yes. So?"

"What makes you think you can take off to Central America and leave your family like that?"

"I'm not sure I have a good answer for that."

"Isn't it a little irresponsible?"

"I suppose it could be seen that way."

"What do you mean it *could* be seen that way; it *is* that way."

"Well, that's your point of view."

"I just don't understand why you're doing this. How are you going to afford it? You don't even have a job."

"Exactly."

"What do you mean, *exactly*?"

"Well, you're right. I don't have a job. Therefore I don't have a boss to tell me I can't do it."

"Well, yeah, I suppose that's true. But how can you leave your family like that? Your wife must be pissed."

"On the contrary. She's excited for me. In fact, it was her idea."

"Her idea! Really? Why would she let you do something like this?"

"Well, first of all, she is not *letting* me do anything. We don't *let* each other do things; we support each other. Like I said, it was her idea. She wants me to be happy; that's all she cares about. She knows that traveling makes me happy."

"Well, that's quite something. It seems a bit crazy, don't you think?"

"Maybe. But there is no time like the present to do the things you want to do. You never know what may come next."

"Aren't you scared?"

"Scared of what?"

"Scared that something might happen to you while you're away in one of those crazy countries."

"Well, I've spent plenty of time in countries that are not particularly appealing on the tourist scale and I somehow survived."

"What if something happened to Isabelle or the boys while you are away?"

"The same question could be asked of me at any time; when I was in the office, or out running an errand. In theory, anything could happen at any time. The only difference here is that it may take some time to get back home. I don't even think about those kinds of things, it doesn't help."

"Well, I'm still a little surprised by it all but you sound like you know what you're doing."

"I'm not saying I have it all figured out. I don't know what's going to happen from day to day or moment to moment, but I'm okay with that. I've been given a gift and I have no intention of wasting it."

The two most prominent human needs are the need for certainty and the need for variety. We all want things in our

A Most Improbable Adventure

lives that we derive comfort from, are repeatable and give us the feeling that everything will be okay. Contrasted with this is the need for change. Essentially we get bored with the first need at some point and crave adventure in order to spice things up a bit. I was certainly comfortable in my stable, predictable life, but needed that sense of adventure as well. This particular adventure would certainly push my limits and I was excited to see what would happen.

I had no specific outcomes in mind; in fact I had no idea what to expect, and that was just fine by me. I had heard it said once that when we experience new things in our lives we get stretched, and we never truly return to our original shape. This creates a bigger space for more and more experiences to flow in, experiences that we *feel* more deeply each time. It stood to reason that the adventure I was about to embark on would effectively do the same for me. It would, to some extent, make me different. How could it not?

Clearly there were those in my life that thought I was doing something foolhardy and rather irresponsible. Who leaves a wife and two young children behind to go gallivanting around the globe anyway? What kind of nut does something like that? Evidently *I* would be that kind of nut. On the other hand I was given the gift of time by my most recent employer and I was not about to squander a minute of it because what I was about to do made *other* people uncomfortable. It's interesting how people's fears become so visible when presented with someone else's ideas. Their reactions tell you what they are afraid of as they dump their insecurities on you. This is how many such adventures get squashed; well-meaning people in your life tell you all the reasons you should *not* do something – and very often you listen.

You never know when you'll be given a gift so you have to have your eyes open to spot it when it happens and be open to receiving more. This was definitely a gift; a release from a situation that was destined to fail. A detour was thrown in my way – sudden unemployment – and I needed to navigate it. I chose to go big in the face of perhaps the most ego-crushing event one can have. I simply said, "Thank you for this opportunity."

If I returned home with nothing more than a bunch of pictures and interesting stories then it would be pictures and stories I would not have had if I had hidden out behind my computer frantically pitching my resume at a random smattering of job postings. I expected, of course, I would have more than that – I just didn't know what. Much like with my world trip a few years earlier I had no idea what I was getting myself into but felt it was the right thing, and the best thing, to do.

I knew I would be running into fellow travelers that would be half my age who wouldn't have a clue about my way of life as a married man with children and a mortgage. As odd as the idea was I welcomed it. In fact, I hoped it would enable me to reconnect to that youthful side of myself that had wanted to travel more in my younger years.

I considered myself to be well traveled. I had been to dozens of countries over the years and seen and done some amazing things. I had experienced plenty of bucket list moments and lots of *get me the hell out of here* moments too. When I look at a globe I'm drawn to certain areas, naturally pulled toward some of what the world has to offer in the way of history, physical beauty, and points of clear differentiation from where I was born, raised, and lived. An area of the world for which I had a few bucket list items, though generally not very high on my overall list, was Central America. I knew it would be a difficult place to travel, especially as a man in his forties who had experienced a level of comfort in life that would be in stark contrast to what I would likely see and experience. It was for this reason I decided Central America was the place to go.

My knowledge of the region was limited, both in terms of its history and current circumstance. The feedback I got from people when I told them where I was going was not very supportive. Just as I had received looks of shock and horror from friends and family many years ago when I told them that I was going to Colombia, most people thought of Central America as an unstable region run by drug lords and crazed military dictators. Their depth of thinking essentially ended at that point. There was no further understanding of the region's current place in the world or whether any of what they perceived to be true actually was. To strike up a conversation with someone about Central America was to ensure a very brief one. Awareness and understanding were truly limited. Mine was not much greater, though I certainly had a more open mind about finding out. Other than lazing on the beaches of Costa Rica none of my friends or family had ever actually spent any time in the region.

Growing up and going to school in the 1970s and 1980s the focus of my public school education in social studies and politics was on Canada and the United States, as well as an in-depth look at the history of Europe. It didn't really extend beyond that. Central America was really just a jumble of countries on a map – there was no discussion about it, no textbook references, no historical analysis. In my young mind it was really just a mass of land that held North and South America together.

That said, what I do recall from those days was hearing on the news about some goings on in places like Nicaragua, largely because of U.S. involvement and battles they had undertaken around the globe against the scourge of communism. Growing up in the Cold War era ensured that dinner time news commentary was heavily laden with updates on events in countries around the world that had communist regimes in place, were considering a left-wing alliance, or even knew how to spell the word communism. I remember thinking at the time how difficult it must have been for the U.S. government to govern their own country when they had their hands in so many pies around the world, trying to save everyone.

I recall hearing names like Daniel Ortega in Nicaragua and Manuel Noriega in Panama and trying to piece together what, in my mind, was a map of chaos and destruction in that tiny zone between North and South America. For such a small area it seemed to garner a lot of attention in the press back then. Whether it was dictatorships, drug trafficking, communism or social unrest, the news was hardly positive. Competing news stories during my youth included the Soviets invading Afghanistan, the Iran-Iraq war, and the Israel-Lebanon conflict, to name just a few. As a young person it was all quite a lot to take in and a lot to process. The world, it seemed, was a dangerous and unstable place.

Ever since I was very young I had wanted to travel and explore the world despite the potential dangers that lay outside the borders of my seemingly safe and secure homeland. It intrigued me to no end to know what different lives we all led even though we were, in some cases, right next to each other on a map. It was this interest that led me to become a traveler and to finally, after many years of deliberation, take a massive and life-altering trip around the world – a trip that did not include Central America. Because I knew relatively little about the region I was intrigued to discover it now. I wanted to somehow integrate it into my consciousness. Just as one can never really know what it is like to be a parent until you become one, I could never really understand Central America without going there.

It was with interest and intrigue painted with trepidation and anxiety that I set off for the uniquely situated jumble of countries that make up Central America. Before getting there, however, I had one very important stop to make first.

VOICES DEPARTED

Other than a three-night stay at a hostel in Mexico City upon arrival and a return flight home from Panama City I had absolutely nothing booked. Part of me was uncomfortable with the idea of having no plan or itinerary. Another part of me liked it very much. I'd been living a rather structured life, especially with two very young children, where schedules were literally everything. For me, the difference between insane and *normal*, such as it was, was one good night's sleep away.

Sitting on the tarmac at Toronto's Pearson International Airport for an hour was not what I had in mind to start my trip but as with most things travel related it was not within my control. As I looked out the window at the hazy Toronto sky I still didn't really know what I was getting myself into. I wrote a card for Isabelle and gave it to her before I left. In it I wrote that I felt something great would come from the trip; I just didn't know what that great thing was or what form it would take.

After an uneventful flight I made my first mistake within minutes of arriving in Mexico City. In an attempt to feel *ready* for my stay I went to exchange some of my U.S. dollars into Mexican Pesos. I did this by getting in line at the foreign exchange kiosk before exiting into the main concourse area of the airport. Now, everyone knows this is the worst place in an airport to exchange money; the rate is typically extremely unfavourable and they tend to trap "rookies" (was I really a rookie?) into thinking this is the best and easiest place to exchange money. You don't want to go out on the street and try to exchange money, do you? Regardless, I stupidly coughed up my coveted U.S. money for some flimsy Pesos only to find a much better exchange rate available at countless other kiosks on the other side of security as I exited. I felt rather silly but it was my first jolt back into the life of being a traveler after a prolonged absence. I did, however, engage in an exchange of a few words in Spanish with a beautiful young Mexican woman at the kiosk. Somehow that made the whole experience less painful.

Jorge, my cab driver, was a friendly fellow who tried extremely hard to keep me entertained as he drove, pointing out where we were and what was coming up around the corner. It actually kept my mind off of things so I suppose he did a good job. After a short while we arrived at the hostel I had booked. Just the sound of it seemed ridiculous to me; a 41-year-old man was staying at a *hostel*. What the hell was I thinking?

I checked in, dropped my backpack and headed out to one of the main streets near the hostel, Madero Avenue, in search of absolutely nothing but the experience. After gaining my bearings I simply noted the approximate locations of stores and restaurants that I knew I was likely to visit during my stay. As I walked I threw random glances down side streets in each direction. That's when I caught sight of it, the unmistakable green circle of Starbucks. I locked in its location into my mental GPS, knowing it would be an important spot for me in the coming days. Feeling satisfied with my brief exploration I headed back to the hostel and fell into bed.

The streets were quiet the next morning at 7:00am. After the cacophony of noise the previous night coming from just outside the extremely thin sliver of glass that masqueraded as a window in my cavernous room I expected things to be hectic and crazed that morning. Perhaps it was just too early. What startled me beyond the decided lack of humanity at that hour was that those who braved the still dark morning appeared to me to be rather over-dressed. Did they think it was cold? Was there a need for long pants, sweaters, jackets, and even toques? Mexico City in late August was *not* cold from my point of view. That said, given its high altitude, it was not particularly hot either. Being from Canada it seemed to me a very comfortable temperature to wear much less than what I saw others wearing.

I made ready to head out to my first important stop of the day – Starbucks. It was a sanctuary of comfort and privacy on my round-the-world trip a few years prior so I was drawn to it, often unconsciously. I certainly didn't think of myself as one of those travelers who sought out the familiar when away from home, like the classic tale of a North American teenager seeking out the grease-infused golden arches of McDonald's while on a school trip to Europe. I did, however, think of myself as someone who knew what he liked and, fortunately or not, the café mocha at Starbucks was something that I liked.

Stepping up to order I quickly scanned my limited database of Spanish words and pulled together something resembling a sentence: "Quesiera una café mocha alto por favor." A brief moment of pride overcame me as I realized I had just communicated to someone in Spanish. My chest expanded, a smile cracked my face, and my heart rate slowed as the tension that had built up began to dissipate.

My moment of glory, however, was shattered like the unsuspecting windshield of a car when a rock, propelled by an enormous cargo truck, smashes into it. I suddenly realized that I normally order it with non-fat milk. How the hell was I going to communicate "non-fat" to the barista? My heart rate jacked up again. I began to sweat a little in anticipation of the uncomfortable exchange where I would show that I am, in fact, a jackass who knows virtually no Spanish.

There was nothing I could do but say "Como se dice non-fat milk?" in hopes that the staff there had had enough tourists come through asking the same stupid question that they would not only have the answer but also appreciate that I preceded the English words in my question with Spanish ones. Fortunately, the young woman behind the counter smiled and said "Leche light." Relieved, I repeated "Leche light." There's nothing like a little Spanglish—a word or words created by the smashing together of English and Spanish—to make a guy feel better about his lack of foreign-language vocabulary and proficiency.

It was going well, I thought. I had ordered my drink, got it with non-fat milk, and was ready to pay. Then my moment of pride was rocked again. This time by the inevitable question I always get: "Would you like whip cream on that?" Of course, the question came out of the girl's mouth as a barrage of sounds that made absolutely no sense to me whatsoever. I should have known the question was coming but in the moment I simply froze, unable to comprehend what had just happened and unable, it seemed, to generate any words or form any type of coherent sentence. My brain sat, paralyzed, unsure of what to do. I was the proverbial deer in the headlights, looking rather wide-eyed and stunned. Thankfully she brought me back from the edge and said "Whip cream?" I quickly replied, "No gracias."

Now I'm good, I thought. I was wrong, again, of course. "Como te llamas?" she inquired. My limited Spanish vocabulary and my vast Starbucks experience came together in an instant on the spot and I quickly responded "Jason." She promptly asked again what my name was, as she likely did not hear it often. I repeated, twice, knowing that it really didn't matter as there were not dozens of people clamouring around the bar waiting for coffees of a similarly detailed and complex description. I would respond to anything even remotely close to my name that was called out. She scratched something on the cup that I assumed would approximate J-a-s-o-n, which I spelled again for her, in Spanish.

Finally I had completed the ordering process. I had successfully ordered a café mocha in Mexico City; what a relief.

A Most Improbable Adventure

When I received my drink I saw how she had spelled my name: J-e-i-s-i. Close enough, I thought. At least she drew a smiley face on the cup. I sat and relaxed and ever so slowly drank my elixir, pondering life and my upcoming adventure.

Afterward I made my way to a pickup spot where I would meet a shuttle bus that would take me to Teotihuacan. I had wanted to go to the ancient city of a long-since disappeared civilization not far from present-day Mexico City for many, many years. I was reminded of the speed of things in Mexico as I waited nearly an hour for the shuttle bus to arrive carrying my fellow *touristas*. At the head of the bus was a tiny young man in dress pants and suit jacket. His black hair was slicked back and his bright teeth shone against his dark skin. He couldn't have been more than 22-years-old but he was to be our guide for the day. His real name was a convoluted combination of at least five names strung together like a Christmas wreath so he asked that we simply call him Alan; so we did.

Alan asked that we all quickly introduce ourselves. On board the shuttle bus were two young girls from Denmark, two studs from Italy, a very dark-skinned girl from Germany, a couple from Guadalajara, a rather studious looking young man from Monterey, a young woman from Australia and a pasty-white couple from England. From that point on Alan referred to us by our country, not our name. Countries were easier to remember, he reasoned. Amazingly, or perhaps not so in today's global society, everyone spoke English, with the exception of the couple from Guadalajara. Alan repeated everything he said in both languages so I was able to pick up some of what he was saying as he described the passing scenery in Spanish.

Despite his young age Alan seemed to have an encyclopedic knowledge not only of Mexico but other countries as well. I supposed he had had enough visitors from countries around the world that he questioned and learned from that he was able to explain something about every country represented in the bus. He knew that Toronto was Canada's biggest city,

11

Ottawa was the capital, and that Stephen Harper was a rather unpopular Prime Minister. I chuckled at that one.

The day would be spent making our way to the main dish: Teotihuacan. Fortunately I knew it was going to take a while to get there and I also knew we would all be pushed into the forced selling environments I had become so accustomed to in other countries around the world – especially Egypt and India. Alan entertained us along the way with a sharp wit and outgoing personality. His energy and exuberance defied his tiny frame.

At Tlatelolco I learned that it was the twin city to Tenochtitlan, the ancient Aztec capital that would eventually become Mexico City. Tenochtitlan eventually annexed, or overthrew, this sister city and took it over completely. The city sat on an island in a large lake and had bridges to the mainland at the four cardinal points. The ruins at Tlatelolco showed where the island and mainland connected. Over the course of time the city grew bigger and bigger and eventually the entire lake was drained, save a few small ponds in the south part of modern-day Mexico City.

I also learned of the approach the Spanish took in their attempts to convert the locals to Catholicism. They destroyed the temples and used the rubble, mostly volcanic rock, to construct their churches. In this way they tried to convince the Indians that their religions were really not that different – after all, the building materials of the church were the same as their temples. On this site the Spanish built Iglesia de Santiago in 1512, believed to be one of the first churches built in North America.

The construction of Aztec temples followed an approach whereby the initial temple, a pyramid, was built upon successively every 52 years—coinciding with the Aztec century—thereby encapsulating the smaller temple underneath the newer, larger one. A calendar year consisted of 13 months of 20 days each. After 52 years had passed they celebrated the turn of the century and added another layer to the pyramid temple. This meant that when the Spanish destroyed a temple they effectively peeled a very, very large onion. Each time they pulled a layer off they found another temple beneath.

One of Mexico City's main attractions is the Basilica of Our Lady of Guadalupe. I was struck initially not by its beauty but by its slant. As with everything in Mexico City it was built on the aforementioned lake—Lake Texcoco—and therefore it had sunk about fourteen feet into the ground. The main plaza sloped down dramatically toward the entrance of the Basilica. I felt off balance as I approached it.

It was, in fact, closed for twenty years in an effort to stop the subsidence. The substructure was reinforced but they thought better of trying to actually raise it up to level again, not wanting to risk further damage. The chapel to the side of the Basilica had suffered the same fate, having physically separated from the Basilica it listed significantly to the right as viewed from the plaza.

A new Basilica, built nearby in 1976, was primarily constructed to house the cloak that a native-American peasant by the name of Juan Diego was wearing the day in 1531 when he encountered an apparition who identified herself as the Virgin Mary. Her image miraculously appeared on Juan Diego's cloak and is the reason that the Basilica is the most visited Catholic pilgrimage site in the world. The modern Basilica was a more secure location where even more pilgrims could see the cloak. In its original location it would take hours for people to view the cloak because the lineup was straight out the door and thousands of people deep. Many pilgrims traveled the distance within the Basilica on their knees; not only a painful proposition but a logistical challenge to be sure. In the new location the cloak can only be viewed for a few seconds as you pass by on a movator – a moving walkway.

As I took the brief trip of about fifty feet going one way I couldn't get a great view so I waited to come back the other way. Had I chosen to I could have done the trip two more times as the moving platform had four rows – two going one direction and two going the other. I noticed a flashing red sign nearby that said "No flash photography." I noted this to Alan and the others, the fact that a flashing sign was saying "No flash photography," and they all chuckled; demonstrating some level of comprehension of my sometimes weird sense of humour.

"You have a good attitude, Canada," Alan offered in reply.

"You have a good attitude, too," I replied.

I took the opportunity to chat with Alan.

"How long have you been a guide?" I asked.

"Three jeers," the 'y' sounding more like a 'j'.

"Do you do the same tour every day?"

"No, I do a different one nearly every day."

"Do you like it?"

"Yes, berry much," the 'v' in 'very' being taken over by the 'b' sound.

"Well, you seem to like it. I can tell that you enjoy talking about these things."

"Gracias, Canada. I'm glad you can see that."

"Indeed I do."

As we walked back to the bus I struck up a conversation with Fernando; the tall, handsome and studious-looking Mexican that reminded me a bit of Clark Kent.

"What are you doing here in Mexico City?" I inquired.

"I'm here to do some government paperwork," he replied in perfect English.

"You had to come all the way to Mexico City to do it?"

"Yes, unfortunately, this is the only place I can do it. I've come for a couple of days so I decided to hang around and do some tourist stuff," he said, adjusting his glasses.

"Tell me, where did you learn to speak such excellent English?"

"I studied English in Canada, actually."

"Really? Where?"

A Most Improbable Adventure

"In Montréal."

"That's cool. My wife is from Montréal."

"Really? I spent three years in Montréal, and also some time in New York City after I graduated."

"Wow, that's amazing. What do you do now?"

"I work in the wine industry. I have a firm that provides consulting services to wine producers."

"That's pretty amazing. You studied in Canada, worked in the U.S. and now live in Monterey. Did you pick up French when you were in Montréal too?"

"Yes, a little bit. My studies were in English but I had friends there who spoke French of course."

"That's very cool, and rather impressive. If you don't mind my asking, how old are you?"

"I'm twenty-seven. I know I look young."

"Not only do you look young, you *are* young!"

"Not *that* young. How old are you?"

"I'm forty-one."

"What? You don't look forty-one at all. You look more like thirty-one."

"I hope that's true when I'm fifty-one also!"

We continued to chat about all manner of topics. Including his various travel adventures and, of course, I shared some of mine too. I could not get over how such a young man had done so much. It was people like him that made me wish I had done more in my early years. I could get over the fact that he was about 6-foot 4-inches tall and could easily be a model but I had a slight tinge of jealousy for his having studied and worked abroad and his command of two, almost three, languages.

Back in the bus on the highway I started to notice a different landscape outside of my window. I asked Alan about it. He informed me that we were traveling through what he called the poverty belt. The poverty belt provided a stark contrast to the rest of the city. Although it wrapped itself around the city it appeared to be a very different place altogether. Literally just outside the city limits it is home to 17 million of Mexico City's twenty-five million souls; if not more. The ramshackle homes covered the hills around the city and continued to spread unabated for as far as the eye could see. The homes were primarily concrete boxes stacked on top of and beside one another and nearly all were a dull grey in colour. Alan explained that the reason they were grey is that until homes are painted they are deemed to be incomplete, and therefore exempt from paying property taxes. Paint was not all that lacked on most homes; a deficiency of some ilk was prominent on almost every box – a missing window, door, or even a roof. It was apparent that exposing one's home to the elements, and neighbours, was preferable to paying property tax. An interesting trick, I thought.

These houses started popping up in the 1960s and their growth has continued steadily since, hence the seemingly endless supply scattering every hillside in sight. Originally they were set up as a means to an end by the government: they provided the building materials to the locals in exchange for votes. The locals of course could care less about the value of a vote but they did have some concern over building materials and the ability to actually construct their own home. It was an easy trade to make. The result is a mass of ugliness that I'm sure would be visible from space. The government at one point, according to Alan, decided that they, too, disliked the poverty belt and thus pulled in the city boundary such that it ended at a more pleasant location, putting the poverty belt officially outside of the city. In this way Mexico City dropped off the list as the most populous city in the world. What is in or out of the city is semantics of course as it is all just one big jumble. The locals, however, still used vernacular like "commute into the city" even though they may sit only blocks outside the legal boundary. Whether or not any of this was true almost didn't matter – it made for good content in Alan's lengthy tale.

A Most Improbable Adventure

Upon arrival at Teotihuacan I found myself taking a few deep breaths. I was reminded of my arrival at Giza and seeing the Pyramids for the first time. It was awe-inspiring then and I felt a sense of wonder now as my stomach fluttered. I also quickly flashed back to the annoying hawkers and touts at Giza and hoped that Teotihuacan would be different.

After having seen pictures of the Pyramid of the Sun, Pyramid of the Moon, and Avenue of the Dead many times I was thrilled to finally be there. The massive expanse of the place was accentuated by the decided lack of tourists; traveling during low season had some benefits, it seemed. Though there were few hawkers they were persistent. I felt a little like a fish being dropped from a bucket into piranha-infested waters. Every conceivable knick-knack was offered, including various head-dresses and even noise-making devices that created jaguar-like growls. I had little interest in such things of course so I gave only a subdued wave to everyone who stuck something in my face as I passed, gently saying "No, gracias."

I looked straight up as I faced the Pyramid of the Moon, following the lines of the steps as my eyes rose. I did it slowly, so as not to miss a single step. I felt slightly dizzy by the time my eyes rested upon the summit. Though others rushed past me and started the climb up I just stood there, motionless, taking in the energy that seemed to radiate from the ancient rock. I closed my eyes and breathed deeply, taking in the heat and moisture in the air into my nostrils. I'm not sure how long I stood there. Then, finally, I started the climb.

I pulled out the one trick I knew of climbing up steep steps such as those in front of me: the zig-zag approach. While hiking the Inca Trail to Machu Picchu years before I had learned that it was easier on the legs to walk in this pattern rather than try to go straight up. It worked wonders on the trail, saving my legs from burning even more than they did or giving out altogether. It also helped to not put so much pressure on the knees. Recognizing that I was actually strategizing about how to climb a pyramid suddenly made me feel my age. Was anyone in their twenties putting this much thought into it? Despite maybe over-thinking it I immediately started going up in a zig-zag pattern, aiming first to the left and when I ran out of space turning to the right and aiming in a straight line again. Before I knew it I had reached the lookout area, which, sadly, was not on the summit but perhaps two-thirds of the way up. I barely broke a sweat from the actual exertion even though it was a warm and cloudless day.

Before I turned around to take in the view I closed my eyes, reached back into my memory and pulled out the picture I had of that view down the Avenue of the Dead. I don't know why I did this – the view was right behind me, why would I try to conjure up the image in my mind first? It's almost like I wanted to do a comparison, a reality check. In some way I couldn't believe I was actually there – maybe that had something to do with it. Maybe it's a bucket list thing; the need to double-check and make sure the reality is, in fact, consistent with our expectations.

Slowly I turned, breathing deeply, and finally, gently, opening my eyes, initially gazing low, toward the plaza immediately below me. It was like a broad and empty parking lot, save the single-step stone structure in the middle, like a belly button on a giant abdomen. Surrounding the plaza were several small four-step pyramids—each surely with its own function and story—providing an impressive frontage to what must have been an enormous meeting place nearly two thousand years before. My eyes then drifted upward, looking south and taking in the seemingly endless avenue as it ran off into the distant mountains on the horizon. The bulk of the Pyramid of the Sun grabbed my attention on the east side of the avenue, its great height in turn dwarfed by the mountain immediately behind it in the far distance.

My gaze fell and back-tracked along the avenue all the way to the plaza below me. As I stood there I realized that the view

A Most Improbable Adventure

was indeed almost exactly the same as the one in my mind, with only one difference – I now felt part of the picture. I was *in* it, not *observing* it. I was part of the landscape, as though someone else had painted me into the image. As I took in the vastness of it all my head became heavy and I almost lost my balance. I sat down and hung my head deeply, breathing in and out slowly and methodically. With my eyes shut tightly I felt like I was floating on the warm breeze that rushed past my ears. I listened carefully. Did I really hear whispers or was I just imagining things?

I opened my eyes once more and took in the broad landscape. Yes, it was still there. I closed my eyes again and slowly repeated my mantra to myself. I felt as though I was sinking into the stone on which I sat. My eyes still closed, I thought I heard a familiar voice. Could it be? Was it Earl? My heart leapt.

THE MUSEUM IS CLOSED

In the spring of 2012 the news was bad. My brother Colin's best friend Earl's health had taken a turn for the worse. In the previous ten years Earl had made dramatic changes in his life to accommodate his condition – an aortic dissection – a relatively rare disorder in which the inner wall of the aorta tears and one that typically occurs in men nearly twice his age. Actor John Ritter died of the same condition in 2003. As a result of his illness Earl, at the age of only thirty-seven, was forced to stop doing nearly everything he loved to do. No more rock climbing, no more hockey, no more basketball, no more of anything that would elevate his heart rate beyond a safe zone.

Both Colin and Earl were passionate about life, wanting to live it fully. They weren't crazy, at least not completely, they just loved to do things they cared about and they wanted to learn things, constantly. Colin had been a tremendous role model for me as I grew up, largely because of this. He was the least sedentary person I knew. When he told me that Earl had developed a very serious condition, and that it would dramatically reduce his activities, I was shocked. Taking away Earl's pursuits effectively took away Colin's because they did nearly everything together for their entire lives.

Earl was a trooper. He made all the necessary changes and, in his usual style, picked up new things. That was Earl, pouring himself into everything he did. He would decide one day that he wanted to learn to do something new and before long he would become an expert. He'd then need a new challenge so he would stop—cold turkey—whatever he was doing and pick up something new. Much of his life was spent doing exactly that.

He was otherwise in good health for nearly ten years. Then his body started to break down. After innumerable surgeries his spirit simply decided it was time to shed that particular garment.

Having been best friends with Earl since the age of five Colin's loss was great – like the loss of a brother. When Colin called that night to tell me that Earl had passed I was stunned. The energy drained out of me. I sat silent on the phone searching desperately for something, anything, to say, but nothing came. I felt Colin's pain deep in my heart and I knew he was absolutely consumed in anguish yet I could still not form any words. He had lost what to him was his brother and I, ultimately, had lost a piece of mine.

The funeral was, without a doubt, the most uplifting and fun-filled service I had ever experienced. Earl had friends in many areas of his life and they had come to celebrate, not mourn, him. Jokes were cracked, stories were told, and even skits were performed. There were tears of course, especially when Colin shared his many memories of Earl. Colin's children were all there, tears streaming down their faces. It was gut-wrenching.

I had flown home for the funeral and very much wanted to spend several extra days to be with Colin. During those days we were nearly inseparable. We went for coffee, lunch, dinner and then talked more after his kids had gone to bed. It was the most time we had spent together in over a decade. I had missed him, and I wanted to be there for him when he needed it most. I learned a great deal about Earl over those few precious days – and I learned a great deal about my brother as well.

About a month after the funeral I lost my job. As I reflected on my situation, as seemingly tough as it was at the time, I

A Most Improbable Adventure

thought of Earl. *Holy shit, he was only thirty-seven when his life changed due to illness. That's so young, too young. Now he's gone. I'm forty-one; something like that could happen to me at any moment.* As the days passed I kept thinking about how fragile my life was and how little control I truly had of it. I also thought about the gift I had just been given – time.

The loss of a job is never a fun thing. In fact it hurts. It's especially damaging to the ego. In a way, however, I felt as though I had just escaped something ominous, even if it wasn't explicitly my choice in the moment. I suddenly had what everyone wanted – freedom. There is something exciting about the idea of freedom, of endless possibilities. Choices were suddenly mine and I could do whatever I wanted, whatever made me happy. I could pursue joy, happiness and fulfillment or I could pursue a currency with which to pay my bills.

True, I had escaped, though it was really only a job. I had not, however, escaped death – and my clock was still ticking, seemingly louder now. My ticket for this earthly life-trip could get canceled at any moment. I asked myself whether now was the time to wither away, play it safe, and live small. Should I be conservative, get back on the horse and attempt to make ends meet for my family? That is, do the *right* thing; do what was *expected* of me? What was my alternative? I continued to think of Earl. I also thought about my two young sons. Would they understand that daddy went to get another job? Would they care? Would it make a difference?

The answers were clear. My boys would not understand, would not care. To them daddy was just daddy and that was all that mattered. What I should aim to be is the best me – so they could get the best daddy possible. Would I tell them later in life about that job I got after that other job or would I tell them about that amazing trip I took, pursuing my life-long passion? Which would they identify with more? Which would influence them more and tell them more about their daddy? My choice was obvious. I briefly doubted myself. I wavered a bit. Ultimately, however, I embarked on this most improbable adventure.

I'm not sure how much time passed as I sat there on the Pyramid of the Moon with my eyes closed before I began to sense a presence, something stronger than the whispers. I tried to ignore it, but ultimately gave in to my curiosity. My concentration shifted. One voice became many. It was not Earl, nor the ancients, speaking to me. What I heard were the garbled cackles of a group of Japanese tourists, all shuffling around trying to get the best possible pictures of the avenue below. My moment was over.

As I walked the seemingly endless avenue with my head down I looked at the ground as it passed by wondering who else had walked there and what their lives must have been like. I have always felt a sense of connection to ancient sites in this way, asking questions of people long dead to see what it must have been like to be there way back when. It gives me a sense of understanding somehow and a sense of comfort as well. As I walked I was periodically hunted down by a hawker with some wonderful artifact to sell me and I was forced to give them the bad news as I tilted my head to the side and pursed my lips slightly, giving a sympathetic look along with a gentle "No, gracias." I enjoyed the walk, the solitude, and the somewhat odd sense of connection with the dead.

Returning to the pyramids I stood at the base of the Pyramid of the Sun. As its bulk engulfed my peripheral vision it was clear that it was much larger than the Pyramid of the Moon. It was, in fact, the third largest pyramid in the world. After a rather arduous ascent, fighting the cross-winds and other tourists, I made it to the summit. The wind at the top was thick and heavy and forced me to watch where I was walking much more closely than otherwise. The wind howled in my ears as I circled the summit, taking in an almost 360-degree view; part of it was inaccessible due to some form of construction or repair.

A Most Improbable Adventure

As I looked down onto the avenue below the relatively few hawkers moved quickly to approach tourists as they descended the final steps. It was like watching a video game, with the hawkers playing the part of scavengers jockeying for position in an attempt to harvest the last bits of flesh from the bones of the carcasses, played by the tourists. As I watched this happen an unusual sense of calm overcame me. Normally I got tense in the presence of hawkers and touts as I had dealt with them plenty in my many years of travel but from that height I felt rather removed from it all and was simply the observer.

As I stood in awe looking across at the Pyramid of the Moon a young Indian man gently asked if I would take a picture of him and his wife. He spoke with a British accent and seemed entirely too well dressed for the occasion, his perfectly ironed shirt and khakis flapping in the wind. His wife, a beautiful woman with a nose ring and colourful sari wrapped around her shoulders, stood nearby, flashing me a smile that said thank you before I even agreed to do it. They positioned themselves in front of the Pyramid of the Moon such that it appeared to rest on the left shoulder of the young man. I snapped a number of pictures to make sure at least one would be to their liking. They were a very attractive couple so I would have had to work very hard to make them look bad. They thanked me genuinely and scurried off to begin the descent.

I hadn't thought to ask one of them to take a picture of me so I simply turned on the front-camera feature on my phone and took my own picture. Being old enough to remember when it was necessary to advance the film in a camera I reminisced for a fraction of second and moved on.

Back on the ground and fighting my way through the touts at the base on the pyramid I spotted the Indian couple again. They were, it seemed, heading the same direction I was and were also fighting their way past the jumble of hawkers selling products ranging from the knick-knack to the simply ridiculous. At one point a vendor approached the woman from the side and grabbed her arm to get her attention. That's when the husband lost it. He tore the vendor's arm away from his wife, turned on his heel and stood directly in front of him. A look of rage began to form on the man's face; his wife then moved out of the way.

"What the hell are you doing?" he demanded.

"I can sell this cheap," the vendor replied, as he held out a small statue of the Pyramid of the Sun.

"I don't want your crap and I don't want you touching my wife!"

"No problem, sir," he meekly replied, backpedaling quickly.

The man then muttered something under his breath and stormed off toward the exit. Another vendor, clearly having not witnessed what just happened, approached him. The man made no effort to get out the vendor's way and nearly knocked him over as he hit him shoulder-to-shoulder. He continued muttering something to himself and disappeared up ahead.

I was enthralled with the scene as I flashed back to my own eerily similar experiences in my world travels. I, too, had been pushed to the edge by the constant hassles and even aggressive grabs and gropes and flew off the handle in an outburst of frustration a couple of times in an attempt to create space and catch my breath. What is it about these situations that make it alright to touch a stranger like that? Was the man overreacting? Was the vendor too aggressive? Who's rules should be used, the home team or the away team? It was a vexing question to be sure. So vexing indeed that I decided to simply drop it and move on.

I was the last of the tour group to arrive back at the bus. They were all lounging around under a small stand of trees that provided sparse shade. They all looked tired and worn out from the day's events. In the bus on the way back to the city Alison, whom Alan simply referred to as Australia, began firing question after question at him. Alan also looked a bit tired after a long day of trying to keep us all entertained, his shoulders

A Most Improbable Adventure

slumping somewhat and his bright eyes ever so slightly dull. Clearly she did not pick up on this and proceeded to drill him with questions like Diane Sawyer interviewing the Shah of Iran; it was relentless. I felt bad for Alan.

One tidbit of Mexican life I learned as a result of the barrage of mostly meaningless questions had to do with obtaining a driver's license in Mexico. It turns out that in order to get a driver's license in Mexico all you need is 500 pesos. There is no test to pass. You don't need to demonstrate any skill in a written test nor do you actually have to go out on the road and show that you can negotiate the madness of Mexican streets or highways. You simply need a pulse and a couple of dollars, according to Alan. The exception to this is if you want to drive in the tourism industry. In that case you have to pass a number of tests, perhaps the most important of which is a drug test. Alan attempted to discreetly explain that you must pass a medical exam as well, including a rather invasive anal probe. The bus driver inquired with Alan what everyone was groaning about and when Alan explained it to him he held up his right hand and extended his index finger to give us a sense for what he was subjected to. We all groaned again, the men wincing more strenuously than the ladies.

The following day I attempted to purchase a bus ticket for the long haul from Mexico City to Chetumal, the capital of Yucatán province; a trek I would need to make in the coming days in order to cross into Belize. Though the hostel I was staying at was very modern and beset with various amenities, it was prone to intermittent Internet connectivity, thus making my efforts to buy a ticket online rather challenging. After having negotiated the ticket purchase process nearly to the end I was faced with a page that required I fill in a zip code field; I could not move on until I filled in that field. Sadly, we do not have zip codes in Canada so the page kept denying my ability to move on and complete the sale. I assumed that the bus company thought I must be from the United States if I was viewing their website in English. The alternating alphanumeric format of the Canadian postal code was not the same as the five-digit American zip code so I messed around for some time trying to come up with a suitable zip code. Of course I tried 90210 but that didn't work; it was as though the bus company knew nobody from Beverly Hills would actually take one of their buses. I tried San Diego, San Francisco, even New York, all to no avail. After having exhausted my patience for the experience I did what any normal person would do in a similar situation – I swore profusely at the computer screen and walked away.

I went to the front desk of the hostel and begged for help. Jorge, an unusually helpful fellow, informed me that sometimes similar Mexican websites allow users to get all the way to the end and then suddenly don't accept foreign credit cards – a small offering on his part to appease my anger at having not got past the stupid address page. Jorge took matters into his own hands and actually called the bus company on my behalf. He told me all my options and worked out everything for me, booking my seat in a manner of minutes. Hindsight being what it is, I perhaps should have gone to him from the outset but I didn't want to be one *those* tourists who not only didn't speak the language but was also completely dependent on others. No, I did not want to be *that* guy. Regardless, Jorge saved my bacon and saved me not only more frustration but possibly hundreds of dollars and potential jail time for destroying that computer.

Like a glutton for punishment I went immediately back on the computer to find a place to stay in Chetumal. An hour passed before I gave up and booked something that looked reasonably safe and reasonably priced. It would be one of the extremely rare occasions I would spend anything more than a few minutes online trying to plan ahead on the trip. There was something about just letting things happen that felt better than trying to control things too much. I had given an hour of my life to that dastardly wicked life-sucking force that is the

A Most Improbable Adventure

Internet and I was not about to do it again. In recognition of my small yet meaningful victory I did what anyone else would do – I went to Starbucks.

In front of me in line I overheard a couple from England—at least I assumed they were from England—struggling to order two black coffees. I'm not sure if the cashier was just messing around with them, claiming to not understand that they wanted two simple black coffees, but the couple struggled mightily regardless. Eventually I couldn't take it anymore and I jumped in.

"Do you want just black coffees? That's it?"

"Yes," the woman replied as a look of relief washed over her face.

"How about café negro?" I offered.

She immediately turned to the cashier and said "Dos cafés negro, please." The cashier gave a look of understanding, her eyebrows jolting up and her head nodding in comprehension. With that, all was right with the world.

Moments later, as they looked for the milk container that is usually available on the preparation bar, they discovered that they had neglected to order milk for their coffees. The woman's head dropped in frustration having gone through the painful exercise of finally getting the black coffees she wanted but then realizing they had no milk. She looked at me, expectantly. "Con leche," I replied. She approached the barista and motioned with her hand, as though she was pouring something from it, and said "Con leche." A moment later the couple had their precious milk.

"Are you American?" the man asked.

"No, Canadian," I replied.

"We should know, we just spent a year there," the woman jumped in.

"Really; where?" I asked.

"Banff," she replied.

"Oh, I'm from Calgary so I know Banff very well."

"Nobody is actually from Banff," she rightly pointed out.

"I know. Most people there are from Australia," I noted. They both chuckled.

"How long have you been in Mexico?" she asked.

"I just got here two days ago. How about you?"

"Yesterday."

"Where are you headed?"

"We're going through Central America all the way to Panama City."

"Really? Me too. I only have five weeks to do it."

"We've only got six weeks. We've been in South America for a few months already."

"Fantastic."

"What do you do?" she inquired, seemingly prioritizing this piece of information above nearly all else.

"I'm a travel writer."

"That's great. That's what I want to do – travel writing. Have you written anything recently?"

"I've just written an article for an indie travel site called BootsnAll that talks about the psychology of round the world travel. It'll be published in October."

"I know BootsnAll, that's a great website. I'd love to write something for them. I've been doing some freelance writing, mostly marketing, but I'd love to do some travel writing."

"I think you should."

"I do have a blog going and I'm on Twitter a little."

"Me too. What are your names?"

"I'm Rebecca and this is my boyfriend Greg."

"It's nice to meet you," I replied, shaking both their hands. "My name is Jason. Since we're heading the same direction maybe we'll run into each other again along the way. Let's stay in touch."

"Absolutely," she replied excitedly.

After a quick exchange of contact information we parted ways.

That was the last I saw or heard from Rebecca and Greg from England. Despite the fact that I never saw them again it was still the type of chance encounter that made the travel experience so fascinating for me. What were the chances I would have been at that particular Starbucks in Mexico City at that exact moment so I could meet Rebecca and Greg and come to their rescue with my rudimentary Spanish skills? Incredibly small, I thought.

I pondered the encounter as I continued my walk on Madero Avenue. Only a few minutes later my tranquility was strangled by an approaching cacophony of sounds – a public demonstration of some sort. Hundreds of sign-wielding crazies started marching past me shouting various slogans – some words of which I was able to make out; something anti-government and something that may have had to do with fornicating with one's mother. Whatever it was they seemed rather pissed. Though I was standing off to the side in a storefront doorway I was not clear of the mob. I could have easily been sucked into the passing wave of humanity and been trampled like an insect. After watching hundreds of clearly angry people pass by I decided to make a break for it and attempt to get out of there.

I darted into a side-street and dashed out of sight of the mob, heading in the direction of my hostel. The noise of the demonstration faded behind me as I quickly walked away. I decided right then that it was a good time to visit the Templo Mayor, a major tourist must-see that housed the great temple in the ancient city of Tenochtitlan, and also not far from where I was staying. I negotiated a few more side streets and finally arrived at my destination. Unfortunately the line-up was Disney-long and I didn't feel I had the patience to wait it out. I then made my way to the Mexico City Museum.

The venture was made all the more difficult by the tiny map in the travel guide I was using in that it had mistakenly placed the museum at the corner of 5 Febrero and 16 Septiembre, which it very much is not. Fortunately the address was correct in the text of the guide so I was able to find it, eventually. Unfortunately I did not go beyond the ticket desk because I was informed that the section of the museum detailing the history of Mexico was closed off. As that was the whole reason for my wanting to go there I turned around and walked right back out.

The next day I was the first in line at Templo Mayor and I was the only foreigner in the place the entire time I was there. It was free for Mexicans but foreigners paid full fare, the equivalent of about $5, to visit the ruins and museum.

The construction of Templo Mayor was similar to that of the pyramids at Tlaltelolco and Teotihuacan. A series of successive pyramids were built one on top of each other. Mexico City grew up right on top of the ruins for hundreds of years and nobody knew what was below the surface. The city even built a viaduct right through the ruins about a hundred years ago and they had no idea what they had cut through in order to do so. It boggled my mind.

In the museum there is reference made to Tenochtitlan (Mexico City) being at the axis of the world, geographically speaking: half-way between North and South America and half-way between Asia and Europe. I found this fascinating for some reason. I would not have considered that prior to my visit – why would I? This centre-of-the-world thinking implied that the early Mexicans influenced and were influenced by the other great civilizations of history.

The Mexico City Marathon was in full swing as I exited the museum. As I watched the runners go by I had flashbacks to my own marathon running days. The pained expressions on the runners' faces triggered in me the same feelings I had had when I ran three marathons in an 18-month period a decade prior. There must have been ten thousand people in the square, milling around after their race had finished. Many filtered out of the square and made their way to the multiple McDonald's locations nearby, loading up on questionable food in an attempt to feed their hungry bodies; some made it a

A Most Improbable Adventure

bit further, to the Starbucks, where I ended up. I successfully ordered my café mocha in Spanish, even remembering to turn down the offer of whip cream at the end and spelling my name for the barista to write on the cup. I suddenly felt like a local.

September is the month that Mexico celebrates its independence from Spain. The marathon was just one of many events and celebrations going on in the city. I remembered back to Alan's comments on the tour I had taken a few days prior that most Mexicans did not like Spain because of their harsh rule for centuries but those same people would also be offended if you referred to them as Indian. Somehow the people of modern day Mexico were both and neither at the same time. It struck me how this middle ground could be unsettling – you'd not be sure of where you stood because you wouldn't be sure of where you came from.

Surrounding the marathon route, and on every corner, were armed police in heavy head-to-toe gear, including masked helmets, and carrying black machine guns. Many looked like they were getting ready for a BMX bike race they were so heavily padded. I was surprised to see so many female police officers, especially the older ones with heavy eye and face make-up. I flashed back to my trip around the world and the young girls in the Israeli army I saw in Tel Aviv who wore heavy make-up and carried purses slung over their shoulders along with their standard issue firearm. These officers were most definitely not teenagers however.

I awoke the next morning somewhat anxious about my upcoming bus trip from Mexico City to Chetumal. I had been on many long bus trips in my life but I had never spent a 24-hour period on a bus before and I had no idea what to expect. Getting to the bus station, known as TAPO, was rather painless, a straight shot on the metro bus, so I started to feel a little better. I saw only a handful of other foreigners in the station, reminding me again that I was traveling in low season. As I approached the check-in counter I debated whether this was a good time to practice my limited Spanish or save the gentlemen behind the counter some awkwardness and just jump in with English.

"Hola," I said with a smile. "Habla Ingles?" I inquired.

"Si," he replied, looking a little pissed off. He quickly followed that up with a question for me: "Habla Español?"

I was caught off guard by his rather smart, and somewhat bitchy, retort.

"No. Hablo Español un poco," I stumbled, hoping my effort, as weak as it was, would ensure that he ticketed me through to Chetumal and not Tijuana.

"Where are you going?"

"Chetumal."

"Si, Chetumal. One moment please."

He quickly tapped on his computer keyboard and then passed me the ticket. He then flicked his finger to my right, guiding my eyes to where I would need to check my backpack and stand in line at the gate.

"Muchas gracias," I said, very much grateful for his assistance.

"De nada," he replied, still with a slightly bitchy tone.

I picked up my backpack and made my way to the luggage drop-off. As I did he mumbled something under his breath, in Spanish. Something told me what he said was not exactly "Have a wonderful trip, sir!"

Things got off to a rough start not long after the bus pulled away from the gate. Before we even got out of the yard something wasn't quite right. The bus moved all of about a hundred metres when the driver pulled over. I heard him on the radio saying something that approximated "*problema eléctrico.*" We sat there for nearly an hour as a team of people came out to look at absolutely everything inside and outside of the bus. Eventually they all shrugged their shoulders and conceded that they were not going to be able to fix it. The driver moved the bus forward and circled us back around into the yard. We offloaded and reloaded into a similar bus, though it wasn't as new, or as clean. I slumped down into my seat and immediately missed the extra few inches of legroom I had enjoyed in the other bus. After all the passengers had settled in the bus was off, successfully this time.

I was jolted out of my slumber by the screaming sound of the movie raging above my head. The twelve-inch TV screens, all obscured and impossible to see, played some nondescript Mexican feature, and did so at five times the decibel level necessary to deafen the average person. I tried, but failed horribly, to go back to sleep. The incessant banging in my head stopped only long enough to load another terrible movie before cranking the volume even higher. *This is going to be a rough trip.*

It was at the third or fourth stop—I lost track after a while—as I sat on a bench near the bus that a heavenly voice broke the silence.

"Where are you from?"

I turned, following the wonderful sound, eager to see where it was coming from. My eyes fell on a young woman who had been sitting across the aisle at the opposite window for the entire trip. She had deep, dark, brown eyes and a medium-brown complexion. I guessed she was in her mid-twenties.

"I'm from Canada. Where are you from?" I replied.

"I'm from Belize."

"I'm Jason, what's your name?"

"My name is Joanna."

"It's nice to meet you, Joanna," I said as I extended my hand to shake hers. "I didn't think I'd be speaking English on this bus trip. Are you heading home?"

"Yes. I was in Mexico City visiting a friend for a week. Where are you going?"

"I'm going to Chetumal, staying for a couple of days and then going to Belize City."

"Belize City? What are you going to do there?" she asked as she sat down on the bench beside me.

"That's a great question. I'm not sure yet. I'm kind of going with the flow, not planning too far ahead. We'll see."

"Well, there's not much to see there. You should go to Orange Walk."

"Sorry?"

"Orange Walk," she repeated. To my ear it sounded like '*arynge wahk*' so I asked her to say it a third time, and point to it on my map.

"It's a couple of hours south of Chetumal, more inland, here," she pointed.

"Why would I go there? Is there something special there?"

"Yes. That's where I live."

"Oh. Well, what is there to do there?"

"Lots of stuff. How much time do you have?"

"I have no set time limits. I was thinking a few days, maybe."

"You have to go to Lamanai, one of the best Mayan ruins there is. There are lots of other things to see, too. Plus, you have to stay at the Hotel de la Fuente, my uncle owns it."

"Well, maybe I will."

I, of course, had no plans so why wouldn't I take guidance from a Belizean, seemingly the only one on a bus full of about forty people on a 24-hour journey across southern Mexico? I had one of those feelings in my stomach that said I should just go with what the universe was telling me on this one. My intention was to let the wind blow me wherever it might on this trip so it made sense to follow the guidance of this young woman and just see what would happen.

Having never met a Belizean before, I was curious about her background. I knew of course that the national language of Belize was English but I wanted to know how she came to speak perfect Spanish as well. It sort of made sense, given Belize is surrounded by Spanish-speaking countries, but I was curious nonetheless.

"Creole is my first language, as it is for every Belizean. I learned English and Spanish at home and at school. My spoken Spanish is good but my written Spanish would be incomprehensible."

"And what is it that you do? Are you a student?"

"No, I'm a pharmacist."

"Really? I know I'm never supposed to ask a woman how old she is but I'm curious."

"I'm 21."

My jaw almost hit the ground. I figured she was quite young, but not that young.

"I work in my dad's pharmacy. It's next door to my uncle's hotel. You'll see it when you go."

"Wow, that's pretty cool. You work in your dad's pharmacy. That's very handy."

"How about you? What do you do that you are able to travel like this? Do you work?"

It was an interesting question. I thought about Tim Ferris, author of *The 4-Hour Workweek*, and how he would usually respond to that question. His response was to tell people that he was a drug dealer. That was his way of stopping what he thought was a meaningless conversation about what we "do." I decided a slightly less shocking answer was in order.

"Yes, I work, not in a traditional company or role at the moment, of course."

"Are you married? Do you have kids?"

"Yes, I'm married and I have two boys."

"How old are your sons?"

"My oldest is three-and-a-half and the younger one is eight months old."

"Wow, you have a baby at home and you are traveling through Central America alone?" she said, shifting in her seat.

"Yes, I know it sounds a little crazy."

"Your wife must be very understanding."

"Yes, she's pretty awesome."

Before I knew it the driver had returned and the bus was idling. The other passengers quickly boarded and it was time to leave wherever the heck we were.

After a few more stops along the route (I had completely lost track of where we were and just assumed I would eventually get to where I was going), I was surprised to suddenly be in Chetumal. I had dreaded a day-long trip on a bus but somehow it wasn't actually that bad. Having someone to talk to every few hours helped. Sleeping on the shoulder of a 400-pound man for a few hours wasn't too bad either as he proved to be a much better pillow than the mini blow-up pillow I had brought with me. We were stopped only once by police along the way, much less than I had expected. It was all good, until I stepped off the bus, that is.

A wave of hot, steamy, air punched me in the face as I exited the cool, dry bus and set foot on the pavement at the bus terminal. My nostrils burned with the rotten stench of sewage as it raced into my nose on its way to destroying millions of cells in my lungs. My head literally shot back in an unsuccessful attempt to escape the odour. My eyes burned as though I was sitting too close to a campfire. There was nowhere to go; the stench could not be outrun. I was surrounded. My body slumped as the weight of the hot air gathered on my shoulders. *Welcome to Chetumal*, I thought.

I waited patiently for the young man to unload the bags from the hold of the bus. He was rather casually tossing bags over his shoulder not paying much attention to where they landed, or to the owners of said bags and their concerns over the contents. Finally he reached for my bag. I was excited to get it and get the hell out of there. He ripped it out of the hold and flung it onto the spit-splattered and gum-infested sidewalk. I picked it up as quickly as I could, as though I could save it from picking up the nastiness strewn on the sidewalk – as though it hadn't picked up all sorts of disgusting things in the hold, or in the previous days for that matter. I spotted Joanna and we both went inside the station.

We parted ways with a brief "Good luck" and I was off to find a taxi. I found one quickly outside the terminal and negotiated the driver down by a dollar before leaving. The rancid smell seemed to have subsided somewhat or maybe I was already used to it, I couldn't tell. I had read that Chetumal was not much to look at and therefore my expectations were not high. As each block passed by my expectations were very much met. Restaurants and shops, interspersed amongst car mechanic garages and industrial buildings, were empty and downtrodden. In fact there were hardly any people to be found anywhere. The scorching heat may have had something to do with it but I got a definite utilitarian feel about the place. I knew it would not be a place catering to tourists, which was actually fine by me.

My bearings were completely off so I just trusted that eventually the driver would get me to the motel I had booked. The small Toyota Corolla, circa 1988, rattled and jolted as we launched over every bump and around every pothole. I tried to avoid thinking about the heat and my sweaty clothes, which by that time were clinging to me, nearly dripping. It seemed to me we had driven rather far to get what was supposed to be only a couple of kilometres but I had already negotiated the fare so I wasn't too concerned, other than entertaining for a brief moment the notion that he was taking me somewhere I would be held captive for ransom. Finally I spotted the motel and any anxiety I may have been holding in my body was released. After a day of travel I was glad to know I would soon be resting.

Despite the relatively high price for the room it was not much to behold. It was cool though, to my great relief. The motel was whitewashed, in a Mediterranean style, which proved rather attractive on the website pictures, and that certainly helped to keep the place cool. I knew I was going to be staying in some nasty places on the trip, having reduced my budget significantly relative to my world trip, so it wasn't that bad in the grand scheme of things. I wasn't 18-years-old anymore but I could certainly handle very basic accommodations.

After settling in I went out on foot to explore the city with a photocopied map in hand. I made my way to the esplanade, a tranquil boardwalk along the bay, sometimes referred to as "bay front boulevard." The breeze blowing in off the bay was cool on my hot skin and kept me from overheating. Clearly it was going to take some time for my body to adjust to the temperature change from the high elevation and cool temperatures of Mexico City. The brown water of the bay lapped at the rocks just below the esplanade. I stood and watched as the waves went in and out and then closed my eyes and imagined the water was actually blue.

The reason I wanted to go to Chetumal was to visit the Museo de la Cultura Maya (Mayan Cultural Museum), which was supposed to be fantastic, perhaps the best in Mexico. Chetumal was a natural jump-off point for entry into Belize of course but I really wanted to see the museum as well.

The next day, after sweating off a few pounds walking from my motel to the museum, I noticed it looked a bit deserted. I knew that it was closed on Mondays and it was Tuesday (I thought I was pretty smart to figure that out) so I started to get a bit nervous. The entrance was barred and there was not a soul around. I went to the ticket window but found nothing and no one. There was a sign in Spanish that I roughly translated to say "Construction until April". I supressed the bad words that started to form on my tongue and went to the doors opposite the ticket window, just to double-check. They were locked.

"Closed," came a sound from behind me.

I turned to see a man in workers overalls sitting down near the back steps having a cigarette.

"Is it closed? Está cerrada?" I asked.

"Si. Construction. Closed until April," he replied.

"Until April? The whole museum is closed until April?" I confirmed.

"Si. All museum is closed. Nobody here."

"Okay. Muchas gracias," I replied, dejectedly.

I had learned over many years of traveling to at least triple-check things before giving up. Nothing online had said that the museum was closed for construction. The sign said, I presumed, that it was closed for construction. The cigarette wielding man said it was closed. So I checked the ticket window one last time. I saw another sign, this one in English, and it said it was indeed closed for construction until April. *Shit.* I had spent an entire day on a bus to come to Chetumal so I could go to this museum and it was closed for another six months.

I headed back to the street and asked around, in my broken Spanish, if there was an Internet café in the area. It took several stops before someone was able to direct me to one. I investigated how I would get across the border to Belize and from where I would find a bus or taxi to take me there. I discovered that Mercado Nuevo was the place to go. It was the central market of the city but also where all the chicken buses gathered to take people to other points throughout that part of Mexico and also south to Belize. I had in my mind a fairly modern complex with some sort of order to the buses and their schedule. I turned out to be very wrong.

I felt I was stealing from the taxi driver, paying less than a dollar to take me to Mercado Nuevo. I gave him a tip that doubled the fare; the look of surprise on his face somehow made me feel better. I asked him three times if this was the place to get a bus to Belize and he nodded his head three times in the positive. The market was mass mayhem and though I saw a few chicken buses there was absolutely no order to anything. They parked at right angles to each other and there wasn't an obvious place to buy tickets. I hopped out of the taxi and bumped almost immediately into a group of three backpackers at a taco stand nearby.

"Excuse me, do you speak English?" I asked the tall, skinny, blond guy as we made eye contact.

"Yeah," came a strong Australian accent in reply.

"Do you happen to know where to get a bus ticket to Belize?"

"No, man, we just got here yesterday."

"Oh. Have you seen any signs or anything that would point me in the right direction?"

"Sorry, mate. Like I said, we just got here. Maybe just head over there to those buses and see what you can find out?"

"Thanks. Take care."

"Actually, mate, let me come with you. We may be heading down there in a few days. I'd like to know how it all works too."

"Sure. Let's check it out."

"I'm Craig by the way."

"Jason," I replied as I shook his extended hand.

"Nice to meet you, mate."

"You too. How long have you been traveling?"

"I've been making my way through Mexico for over four months now. My friends over there have been in Mexico for about two months. How about you?"

"I'm making my way from Mexico City to Panama City. I just got here to Chetumal yesterday as well but now I'm heading to Orange Walk, Belize."

"Never heard of Orange Walk, mate."

"Neither had I until two days ago."

"Look, mate. There's a guy getting into that bus. He looks like he might be the driver. Let's check it out."

"Sounds good."

After a brief discussion with the driver, who spoke perfect English, I had secured myself a spot on the bus, which was leaving fifteen minutes later. I said goodbye to Craig and hopped aboard the old 1970s school bus, which still had most of the original markings and warning signs still posted inside. The driver told me it would be $6 to get to Orange Walk, which seemed too good to be true. It turned out to be only six

Belizean dollars, which was only about $3 for me. On board was an interesting mix of people from various cultural backgrounds: Mestizo, Indian, Black, and even white Mennonite farmers. It would prove to be a prelude to the Belizean cultural melting pot I would experience later.

As we waited for other passengers to arrive and get on the bus I thought about my time in Mexico. I thought about getting on a day-long bus trip to travel to a relatively unknown city in order to see what was supposed to be a highlight cultural museum – only to find that it was closed. A smile broke out on my face as I considered how silly it all was. Would I ever be back to that part of the world and try again? Most likely not. Should I be mad about it? Well, I could be, but where would that get me? It's all part of the travel experience – it's unpredictable. Not unlike Forrest Gump's box of chocolates – *you never know what you're gonna get.*

THE FORESTER AND THE FILMMAKER

After paying a ridiculous amount of money for the privilege of *leaving* Mexico our bus rumbled into Belizean territory. I was greeted at the immigration desk by a young black man who could not have been more than 18-years-old. His long frame was slumped over the low, wooden desk in front of him as he shuffled papers and glanced at passports. He was a classic low-talker so I had to ask him three times to repeat himself. He wanted to know how long I was going to be in Belize. I really had no clue but I knew he would need something precise otherwise I'd be standing at that desk for weeks. I said I'd be there for five days and he stamped my passport, handwriting in that I would indeed be there for five days. I guessed I needed to be out before those five days were up or I'd be in some sort of trouble.

The customs official was shuffling people to one of two sides as we all lined up. She may have been the first customs officer I had ever seen with an actual smile on her face.

"Do you have any tobacco or alcohol?" she asked.

"No," I replied.

"Go this way, please," she said, directing me to one side. "Have a great day."

"You, too," I instinctively replied. *Have a great day? Who was this person?* Customs people don't smile. They don't speak. And they certainly don't tell people to have a great day. It felt odd to have someone in her position actually behave in a friendly way. After years of dealing with robots that looked at me like I had committed some horrible crime and then riddling me with their ridiculous questions it was actually off-putting to be treated like someone other than an escaped convict. Not only was her behaviour unlikely, it was improbable.

Upon arrival in Orange Walk I was something short of impressed, especially given the way Joanna talked about the place. I had in my mind a clean, modern and thriving city. As I hopped off the chicken bus I was met by a cloud of dust rustled up from the crumbling, uneven, dirt road. I was at the corner of nowhere and anyplace – one of the random locations the chicken buses dropped people off; there was no actual bus stop. Unfortunately the town was actually not that different from everything I had seen since the border: crumbling roads, toppling shacks, and wild animals running amok.

The Hotel de la Fuente met my modest expectations, though my room had satellite TV, air conditioning, and a small refrigerator. It was clean and appeared safe behind a locked iron gate. I reflected back to my initial conversation with Joanna and smiled at the idea of my being there at that hotel simply because we were on the same bus and she asked me where I was from. Had she not been there, or if we had been on different buses, or any other myriad combinations of things had happened, I would not have been standing there in that room at the Hotel de la Fuente in Orange Walk.

I inquired at the front desk where the best place in town was for a nice dinner. Ivan, the rotund and extremely friendly clerk who looked more Hawaiian or Samoan than Belizean (what the heck did I know, anyway?) advised there were two really good places to eat in town, one very close to the hotel and another called Nahil Mayab (House of the Maya) which was about a ten minute walk. It turned out, as I discovered later, TripAdvisor listed only four restaurants in all of Orange Walk. This was a clue that I was not in a town known for its culinary delights.

Had I not had instructions I'm not sure I would have found Nahil Mayab as the signage in Orange Walk was extremely limited. As I approached what I thought would be the front door I immediately noticed the growth of trees and brush surrounding the property. It seemed odd to see this jungle growth at the corner of two dusty roads that otherwise displayed no vegetative growth to speak of. Ivan had told me there was a patio in the back and that was the place to eat if possible. As I peered through the brush, which acted as a fence, I could see that there was, in fact, a patio that was almost completely covered by greenery.

I was there rather early for dinner so I found myself almost entirely alone, thus a seat on the patio was not a problem. As I walked through the door to the patio I felt the air temperature and humidity drop dramatically. The surrounding gardens provided a green blanket under which to remain comfortably cool. The sounds of chirping birds and a running fountain made me feel like I was at a spa, ready for a massage. I still couldn't believe how beautiful the place was given the rather drab and uninspiring surroundings just outside.

As I browsed the menu I was surprised to see such a broad array of options ranging from common fare like pasta and burgers to Mayan-inspired meals such as Ke'Ken (salted pig's tail in tomato sauce) and Hor'och (corn balls and black beans). I certainly didn't come to Belize to have a burger and fries so I ordered the Hor'och and savoured every bite like it was going to be my last. I'm not sure but I may have uttered a few pleasurable sighs as I ate. I was glad to be alone otherwise I may have inadvertently provided an erotic auditory show for other patrons. A thought popped into my head as I ate: Isabelle would have liked this. She wouldn't have liked much else about Orange Walk but she would have enjoyed a fine and interesting meal in such a relaxing setting.

The next day I mistakenly got up an hour early because I didn't realize that, despite being directly south of the Yucatán, it was an hour earlier in Belize. I felt like a travel rookie again. It gave me a lot of free time to kill before going on an organized trip to Lamanai, a revered Mayan site not far from town. I was picked up at the hotel by a very dark-skinned man in a well-worn pair of jeans and a t-shirt. He sported a golden tooth and spoke extremely fast.

"Hello, sir. It is my honour to meet you and take you on our tour today. My name is Paco."

"Well, it's nice to meet you Paco. My name is Jason."

"We'll be leaving shortly, sir. Please have a seat in the van and we'll be off in a moment."

"Are we picking up more people before we go?"

"Yes sir. We are meeting more people at the boat launch."

"When does the boat leave?"

"Not long, sir. We'll be on our way in a moment."

I could tell that we were not on a tight schedule and *Belizean time* was in effect; that is, we'll get there when we get there and we'll leave when we leave. I hopped up into the front seat of the dusty and broken-down mid-1980s van and closed the door, dust flying up in my face as I did so. A moment later Paco jumped in and started the van with a roar of the engine. I could smell the exhaust immediately. He flashed me his golden-toothed smile and we were off.

As we drove I noticed a small pick-up truck in front of us with three young men in the back sitting on the rail of the truck bed. The driver had on what appeared to be a uniform of some type – army or perhaps police, I wasn't sure.

"Prisoners," Paco said, noticing that I saw the truck.

"What?" I replied.

"They are prisoners. They are being taken to the jail."

"If they are prisoners, why are they just sitting in the back of the truck? They aren't in handcuffs or anything. Can't they just jump out?"

"No, they wouldn't do that."

"Why not? I would think if they had the chance they would jump out and run."

"Not here. There is nowhere to go. When people are caught they will just go to jail and not try to escape."

"Well, that's a little different, not what I would have expected."

"These guys are probably small thieves or maybe they were drunk. They may prefer to be in prison. I'm not sure they would get very far in the jungle anyway."

"Could they get to Mexico or Guatemala?"

"Oh no, they would never last that long."

"Interesting," I muttered, now finished with my line of questioning.

We drove on in silence for a few kilometres before Paco pointed out my window to where we were going. "The river is just over there."

He turned off the road to the right and drove up into what looked like a resort property. There were a number of cabana-like buildings up on stilts. A small boat sat bobbing up and down at the end of a dock. Near the centre of the property was a gazebo with a wooden picnic table tucked away under the shade. Paco instructed me to sit at the table and await the arrival of the other tour members. I grabbed my small backpack from the van and obediently took a seat in the shade at the picnic table.

I sat quietly taking in my surroundings. I tried to figure out if it was, in fact, a resort of some type. A few of the larger buildings could have been tourist cabanas while the smaller ones may have been used for equipment and supplies. I presumed they were on stilts so that they would not be flooded in the event the river overflowed its banks. It was a nice property but it did not seem to be a real resort per se. I couldn't quite put my finger on it. I watched a couple of men working around the grounds, moving boxes and cleaning up the ground around the central building. They didn't seem to be hotel or resort employees and were certainly not dressed as such. I was perplexed.

After a few minutes of observation I called over the older man of the two to ask him a few questions. He was dark, rather overweight, and perhaps in his mid-forties.

"Excuse me, sir," I said, waving at the man, motioning him to come closer.

"Hola," he replied, with a wide smile.

"Could I ask you a question?"

"Of course. How can I help you?" he said in perfectly clear English.

"I was wondering what this place is. Is it a resort or a private property?"

"It's a private property, sir. The tour companies use it to launch their boat trips on the river. Are you going to Lamanai today?"

"Yes, I am. I'm waiting for some other tourists to arrive. So, it's a private property, then?

"Yes, it belongs to an American. He is hardly ever here. I take care of the property. My name is Hermano."

"Con mucho gusto, Hermano. My name is Jason. So who owns the place?"

"It's someone you might know, actually."

"Really? Is it an actor or politician or something?"

"It's owned by John McAfee, the founder of the software company."

"Really? The anti-virus software? He owns this place?"

"Yes, he's never here though. He is usually in Miami and other places. I look after the property for him. I have been here for a long time. I live in that house there," he said as he pointed to the central building.

"What are those buildings over there?" I asked pointing to the smaller buildings opposite what I then knew was Hermano's home.

"They are for experiments."

"What kind of experiments?"

A Most Improbable Adventure

"Mr. McAfee provides money for students to do chemical and geological experiments."

"Is it a university or school of some kind?"

"Yes, something like that. It gives students practical experience."

"Interesting," I replied, still unsure of what actually went on there.

I had since learned that the McAfee property had been raided a few months prior to my visit by Belizean authorities who had suspected that drugs were being manufactured and or sold there. They found no drugs but did find a number of firearms, of which one had no license, earning the eccentric Mr. McAfee a night in jail. Not long after my visit he found himself in hot water again as he was a "person of interest" in the murder of his neighbour at his property on Ambergris Caye, an island located northeast of mainland Belize and home to the popular tourist town of San Pedro. From that point he planned a clandestine escape from Belize into Guatemala, which was successful, though he eventually was nabbed and held in Guatemala City before being deported to the U.S. Interesting, indeed.

Although I was not in a hurry, and clearly had nowhere in particular to go, it seemed an awfully long time before a sparkling white tourist van pulled into the compound. I glanced over at the aged and beaten-up van I came in and then glanced back at what appeared to be about a 14-seat extended tourist van. Their driver did not have a golden tooth but wore a crisp white, collared shirt with the emblem of the tour company prominent on the sleeve and breast pocket. I suddenly felt like I didn't belong—I was the lone traveller who was tagging along with the *tourists* who came with a real tour company in a real vehicle.

Within a few minutes we were all seated in the boat and introduced ourselves to our host and guide, Ignacio, a capable looking young man likely in his late twenties. He fired up the engine of the boat and we were off.

As we made our way down the river Kathy and John from Buffalo, New York provided reality TV-like fodder for us all as she repeatedly barked orders at him, emasculating him in front of everyone. As he struggled to get his camera out to snap a few pictures of the spider monkey we were so lucky to see her voice almost cracked with frustration as it got louder and louder. As he fumbled to get the camera into position for just the right shot that would impress their friends back home she nearly reached out and smacked him with one hand while removing his balls with the other. It was uncomfortable to watch and I'm sure made some of the others feel the same way. Several of the other men squirmed in their seats as they watched a man in his mid-fifties, a thick application of 70 SPF sunblock lathered on his now sweating face, reduced to a child, scolded by his loud and overbearing mother. On behalf of all the men in the boat, and the world for that matter, I just about said something to her but I used some restraint and focused instead on the passing greenery on either side of the river.

Kathy and John had even louder friends with them. I didn't catch their names but they did nothing but bitch about how hot it was. *Really? It's Belize; it's going to be fucking hot.* The woman had clearly spent too much time in the sun over the years as her leathery skin hung from her rack of bones like a wet blanket from a loose clothesline. She still felt it was necessary to point out the obvious heat and complain about its oppressiveness. "This heat is going to ruin my day," she said at one point. I actually felt bad for her, not being able to enjoy the scenery that passed her by undetected.

Mercifully, we arrived at the New River Lagoon and docked our boat. The first order of business was to have lunch – consisting of typical Belizean staples: rice, beans, chicken, and, of course, beer. Most folks went straight to the beer. I chose to sit alone at a table as far away from the complainers as I could find. I created a bit of a social experiment in doing so. Would anyone come and sit beside me? As it turned out I ate very much alone.

"Everyone gather around please," Ignacio said, as loudly as he could without screaming, in order to get our attention in preparation for the tour of the site. "We are going to head out for the tour now. It is important that you stay with the group and that you listen carefully as I will not be repeating myself," he continued. Clearly he had done this tour many times and plenty of those times he surely had people who were busy doing other things, taking pictures, falling behind, or just chatting and not paying attention. He surely had a script and he was not about to repeat it to anyone who was not listening intently. On that note we set off into the jungle to the sound of Kathy's grating voice bitching at her husband to take a picture of absolutely everything.

Lamanai, "submerged crocodile" in Yucatec Maya, is a rather small site by Mayan ruin standards, though it was once a large city at its zenith, home to perhaps 50,000 people, most of who lived on the outskirts of the central city we were then standing in. The shrieking loud sound of howler monkeys reverberated amongst the rocks and trees and seemed to startle a few members of the group. Unless you saw one it was rather difficult to pinpoint their location, their howls seeming to come from all directions at once.

The High Temple, officially called Structure N10-43 and standing 33 metres high, is the highlight of Lamanai, providing a 360-degree view of the surrounding jungle and I was eager to climb it. Many of the others in our group were not in what I would call temple-climbing shape. Ignacio reminded everyone that they did not have to climb it but if they chose to they should go slow and hold the rope. I darted up rather quickly, arriving at the top with a bounce in my step. I looked down to see a very large man struggling to see his feet as he went up, step after labourious step. I called down to him and suggested he use a zig-zag approach as it would be easier on his knees than trying to go straight up. He looked up at me through bloodshot eyes like I was crazy. I encouraged him to try it but he chose to ignore me and continued to put enormous strain on his knees at each step as his excess weight crushed his ligaments. Several minutes later he arrived at the top, breathless and potentially on the verge of a very messy heart attack.

At the top I stood quietly and took in the scene. I breathed deeply and let my mind wander. Thoughts of my family immediately popped into my head. One thing I told my son Sam I would do on my trip was take pictures of his 6-inch high brown teddy bear in all sorts of neat places. I dug into my backpack, held out Teddy at arm's length, and snapped a few pictures using my phone, the treetops spreading out like a lush carpet in the background. I wondered if Sam would understand where I was and how amazing it would be to have a picture of his little teddy bear from such a vantage point. I suspected he wouldn't but I was looking forward to the conversation nonetheless.

Nearing the end of the surprisingly short tour I noticed that three of the group were not with us. They were particularly chatty and often were last to arrive at the next point of interest. I figured they were coming behind us so I waited until everyone else passed on the path and looked back for them. They were not there. I went up to Ignacio and informed him that we had lost three people in the back. He immediately looked pissed off. We waited in an open clearing for a few minutes until it became clear that the others were not coming. We were near the end of the tour so he said we should all go ahead by following the marked path and wait for him at the place we had lunch earlier. He said he would go back and find the others. He was a diminutive and gentle man but at that moment he looked like he could rip someone's head off. His nose flared as he took in deep breaths and his forehead crunched over his eyes.

A Most Improbable Adventure

The rest of us arrived at the meeting point a few minutes later. We waited for quite some time and there was no sign of the group of three and no sign of Ignacio. I then heard a noise coming from the opposite direction of where we had arrived. It was the group of three.

"Ignacio went back to look for you," I said.

"We got lost out there," one of the women replied.

"We waited for you for a while and then Ignacio sent us along and told us to wait. He went back to look for you. He did not look happy."

"He didn't need to go back," replied the man in a southern U.S. drawl.

"Well, he did. I assume he'll be back soon."

We waited for quite some time before we saw Ignacio arrive, his eyes bulging and his breath short. "Where did you go?" he barked.

"We fell behind and came around the other way," replied the man, in a rather defiant tone.

"I told you to keep up with the group. It's important."

"Well, we're here now."

"You should have stayed where you were. Now we are short on time. That's why we have to stay together. Some people have been lost out here for hours. You are very lucky."

"Well, it's no big deal," the man said, almost chuckling.

"It is a big deal." Ignacio was ready to throttle the guy. I could see why. Not only was it dangerous but they were rather nonchalant about it. I was getting pissed off too.

"Well, sorry. We're ready to go now," he replied.

Ignacio turned toward the dock and waved his arm for the rest of us to follow. He was too mad to actually say anything. He stormed ahead and waited impatiently for the rest of us to arrive and board the boat. Just as the last ass touched the seat he bolted the throttle forward and we jetted off. He didn't turn around once or utter a word the whole way back. We arrived in about half the time it took to get there. I had experienced my first Belizean hissy fit. It was kind of fun.

Back at the McAfee property I sat and chatted with Elena, one of the singles on the tour. She was fair-skinned and wore a large sunhat that covered her blond hair and flopped in front of her light blue eyes. She did not return with the others as she had made some arrangements to leave from there by boat and then plane back to San Pedro.

"I detect an accent. You're not from the United States, are you?" I boldly inquired.

"No, I'm from Belarus. I've been living in the U.S. for many years though."

"Where do you live?"

"Seattle. I work for Microsoft."

"How do you like working there, for Microsoft I mean?"

"It's okay. I'm getting a little restless. I really like to travel and I'd prefer to do that more."

"Wouldn't we all?"

"What do you do?"

I should have given the Tim Ferris response – "I'm a drug dealer" – but I decided against it. "I'm a travel writer," I said.

"Cool. That must be great."

"It has its ups and downs."

"Do you write books or articles, or both?"

"Both. I've written one book."

"That's great. What's it about?"

"It's about a trip around the world I took a few years ago with my wife."

"Wow. What's it called?"

"It's called *Around My World*."

"Great title. Where did you go?"

"We went literally around the planet, traveling twice the distance of the circumference of the globe. It's really a travel memoir."

"I'll have to look it up when I get home."

"I hope you do."

A few minutes of idle conversation followed and then her boat arrived. Just like that she was off, heading further up the river and back to her resort.

Back at the Hotel de la Fuente I asked Ivan where I should go for dinner.

"Almost next door is a place called Paniscea. It has great food, and it's owned by a Canadian."

"Very cool. A Canadian owns it, really?"

"Yes, he's in here quite often. A really nice guy named Doug."

"Thanks, Ivan. I think I'll head over there tonight."

Paniscea really was almost next door, just a short walk down the street. It sat adjacent to the New River (Rio Nuevo) and was reached via a small path. The restaurant was really nothing more than an open-air gazebo with eight or ten tables and a bar. Despite the diminutive size of the place I was immediately taken by the gleaming wood of which the tables, chairs, and bar were made. It seemed almost too contemporary, considering the general shambles that surrounded it. I couldn't help but think it would be very expensive given its chic look; again surprising given where it was. I thought maybe it was really nothing more than a tourist trap but as I sat and looked around I could tell that there would be no tourists that night. In fact I was one of only two patrons the entire time I was there.

Within moments of sitting down I saw a tall, white man approach the backside of the gazebo – the kitchen, I presumed – carrying two large boxes. That must be Doug, I guessed. After a couple of minutes he emerged and came right to my table.

"Hi, I'm Doug, the owner of the place."

"Good to meet you, Doug. My name is Jason. I'm staying over at the Hotel de la Fuente. They said I should come here for a great meal."

"Well, I hope we don't disappoint."

"I'm sure it will be great. I understand you are Canadian, is that right?"

"Yes, I am, originally from Regina, Saskatchewan."

"I'm Canadian also. I'm originally from Calgary but I live in Toronto."

"Oh, a fellow Canadian, that's great. Welcome to Belize."

"Thanks, I'm glad to be here. I have to say, I'm intrigued as to how a guy from Regina ends up in Orange Walk."

"That's a long story."

"I've got time."

"Why don't I come by after you've had your meal and we can chat?"

"Great idea. See you shortly."

After my meal I sat there pondering what could have brought Doug there. I made up all sorts of scenarios in my head. He looked to be about my age—maybe he had a health scare, like my brother's best friend Earl, and decided to live a new life in a new country. Maybe he got laid off from his job, like I did, and said screw it to the corporate world. Maybe he was a renegade running from the law.

"How was your dinner," he asked, interrupting my daydreaming.

"Fantastic, I replied, the fish melted in my mouth."

"Glad to hear it," he said. "That fish comes right out of the river over there," he said, pointing over his shoulder.

"It was really good," I continued.

"Do you mind if I sit down," he asked.

"Not at all, please do."

"I've been sitting here wondering how a guy from Regina finds himself in Orange Walk and I've come up with all sorts of potential answers. Why don't you let me off the hook?"

"Sure, of course. Like I said, it's a bit of a long story but I'll try to keep it short," he said.

"No worries," I interrupted, "I have nowhere to be."

"Well, I'm a professional forester and I was working for the Saskatchewan government for many years. I came down to Belize on vacation a number of years ago and really liked it.

A Most Improbable Adventure

Eventually I was coming down a few times a year. On one of my trips down here I heard about how there were hundreds of very old trees lying at the bottom of the river over there. As a forester I was immediately interested in understanding why. I discovered that the British, nearly 200 years ago, cut down the native trees around here and floated them down the river to the sea where they loaded them onto their ships and took them home. While they were doing this hundreds, if not thousands, of them fell to the river bed and most were perfectly preserved. There was a real opportunity there to bring them up to the surface and use them to make all sorts of products. Long story short, that's what I did."

"So you bring these trees, logs really, up from the river bed and work them into things and then sell them?"

"Basically, yes."

"Doesn't the government or anyone else care? Are there some sort of regulation or anything?"

"Yes and no. When I first started this venture there wasn't much I had to do. In fact, the government was happy because I was employing locals to get these logs up. I had a guy running sonar on the river bed, then a couple of divers who would go down and attach winches to the logs, and a couple of guys hauling them out. I'd then either sell them as-is or take them to other shops that would work them into something else. The tables and chairs here in the restaurant are made from logs we got off the river bed."

"Wow, they're beautiful. You said yes and no earlier. Why do you say that?"

"Well, the government that was in power at the time didn't care what I was doing. Then the government changed hands. That's the biggest adjustment for me coming down here was dealing with the politics, it's quite something."

"What do you mean? How is it different than Canada?"

"It's totally different. Here there is a two-party system of alternating favours. When the government changes hands they immediately un-do everything the prior party had done. When I started my business I paid a tiny little fee to get a permit to pull these logs up. When the government changed hands they wanted to charge me thousands of dollars to do the exact same thing. I said thanks, but no thanks and stopped. I knew I wanted to stay here though so I opened up this place instead."

"That's crazy. The new government was basically trying to extort you?"

"More or less."

"Did you consider going back to Canada and just saying screw it?"

"I did for a little while, but I realized I wanted to be here more than I wanted to be there. I just had to adjust to the politics and work within the system. Eventually I came to realize that I could adjust – and I did."

"Wow, that's sneaky politics. I'm not sure I could handle that."

"You know, it's actually not sneaky. In fact, it's right in your face politics. That's the difference."

"What do you mean 'right in your face' politics?"

"In Canada everything is so convoluted and there is so much back room bargaining. Here there is no back room bargaining; there is asking, or telling, and nobody hides. That's what I mean by 'in your face' politics."

"So, theoretically, all you would have to do is wait for the government to change hands again and you could go to the local guy and ask for your old permit to be re-instated?"

"In theory, yes, though I would have to start talking to him a long time before the election. Of course, he knows I want that permit and he likely won't let me have it for a few bucks anymore. He also knows I won't pay thousands of dollars for it. He'll ask me directly to pay a certain amount and I'll say yes or no. It's really different than what you and I are used to in Canada."

"It sure is. I don't know if I could adjust to that."

A Most Improbable Adventure

"That's the biggest barrier to more people moving down here, I think. If you can adjust to the politics, it's a great place to live and work."

"What's your take on the various ethnicities that co-exist here?"

"You know, it all seems to work, for the most part. I guess it's no different than Canada, or anywhere else, where there is a mix of 'local' and outside ethnic groups. The challenge here is that the Chinese seem to be the most targeted for crime. You probably noticed that most of their shops have bars on them."

"I did notice that. Why is that?"

"They've suffered so many robberies and attacks that they basically don't allow anyone into most shops anymore. They serve you through the bars now. You can still buy whatever you want; you just can't go in anymore."

"That certainly is different than back home. What else is different here?"

"Well, people here work to live rather than live to work like we do in Canada."

"What do you mean?"

"Well, people here simply work to provide for the basics, the necessities of life. They don't work themselves to the bone trying to get ahead like people in Canada, or many other places, do. They don't shoot for the stars here and try to become super successful. They just want to put in their time, get paid, and enjoy life. They want to be the same as the guy next door, not better than the guy next door."

"So, what are your plans for the future here?"

"I plan to stay for the foreseeable future. I'm part of this community and I have adapted. I'll probably get back into the wood business and I'll certainly be here at the restaurant. I love the people, the weather, and my life here. I'm not going anywhere."

As I walked back to the hotel I had a strong feeling that meeting Doug was the reason I was supposed to come to

Orange Walk. Had I not ended up chatting with Joanna on that one-day bus ride across southern Mexico I would not have learned of a town called Orange Walk. Had I not stayed at the Hotel de la Fuente, per Joanna's suggestion, I likely would not have found Paniscea and would not have had such a fascinating discussion with a former forester from Saskatchewan who had a vision to make a life for himself in Belize by pulling up 200-year-old logs from the bottom of the river that flowed by only steps away from his restaurant.

Doug, it seemed, did not have a dramatic life event drive him to move to Belize, but more a desire to live a life of fulfillment. He had somehow figured out how to adjust and integrate himself into the community. I got a strong sense from him that he did not wish things were different in Belize. He talked about adapting, not trying to change the way things were. He did not complain about what may have appeared from the outside to be an incomprehensible political environment, he simply adapted and was working within that system. He was not forcing anything. In fact, he was letting life come to him, and it seemed to be working just fine.

Without his knowing it Doug had provided me inspiration. I had come to Central America to explore, to expand my mind and spirit, to take advantage of a gift that was given me, and, ultimately, to seek fulfillment. He showed me that anything is possible.

I had no plan the following day so I headed down to the lobby for the free toast with peanut butter and fruit. I asked Ivan what I should do that day and he said there wasn't much to do in Orange Walk. I decided on the spot I would leave town that day and head for Caye Caulker, an island just off the mainland, about 20 miles northeast of Belize City, and home to probably the second most tourists in Belize after San Pedro. In a way I almost didn't want to go just for that reason. I felt like I needed to go experience the beach scene there lest I feel the wrath of my friends and family as I explained I went all the way

A Most Improbable Adventure

to Belize and didn't go to the beach or go diving or snorkeling. I knew it would be a good place to just relax – something I am traditionally not very good at.

Another chicken bus ushered me down the road from Orange Walk to Belize City, with no air conditioning or particular focus on safety. It was packed with men, women, and children of all shades of colour. Having my backpack with me on the seat afforded me some space for a while until the bus got so jammed with bodies that I eventually had to relent. The seats eventually overflowed and the aisles became full. There must have been a dozen women with at least one very small child in tow. They held the children in their laps or on their hips as the stood, trying to keep their balance as the bus rattled and shook down the road. Though it was the main highway in Belize it was really nothing more than a side road by North American standards, perhaps worse – full of potholes, no dividing line and no shoulder.

The children were all amazingly quiet. They uttered not a sound of discomfort or displeasure over what I thought was very uncomfortable conditions. I couldn't help but think about how I would have traveled back home if I had Will or Sam with me – Will in his stroller and Sam comfortably and securely seated. The children here, though not secured, seemed comfortable just clinging to their mothers. The youngest baby on the bus could not have been more than two months old. Back home you would be ostracized, and possibly imprisoned, for not having your baby restrained in a properly-installed baby seat. I wondered if maybe we were a little uptight in North America or if the rest of the world was just crazy.

As the countryside rolled past I glanced around the bus, just observing. I made eye contact with a tiny little girl of about two years of age. She quietly sat snuggled against her mother's breast, wide-eyed and silent. Our eyes met briefly, just long enough for us to exchange a quick smile and giggle. My heart tugged for just a moment as I thought about my boys. Will was only eight months old and I missed holding him the way many of the mothers on the bus were holding their babies. I missed hearing his tiny little breaths go in and out. I missed feeling his warm little body and soft cheek against mine.

The bus pulled over to the side of the road, a road with no shoulder, at least thirty times along the way to Belize City to let people on or off. Somehow the pair of guys who were taking fares could remember who got on where and how far they were going. By my estimate a hundred people were on the bus at some points in the trip and I could not figure out how they managed to keep it all straight.

The bus driver, a heavy-set, dark-skinned man in his twenties, insisted on thumping extremely loud Spanish-language rap music the entire journey. Not that the quality of the road would allow much rest but the pounding music made it impossible to think. Maybe that was the plan – distract riders with such obnoxious and unnecessarily loud music that they wouldn't notice the rattling old bus, the wire thin seats, the lack of air conditioning or the dozens of stops and starts along the way. The music, combined with the constantly gyrating bus made me nauseous so I had to look out the window and focus on the distant horizon to keep it from getting worse.

After what seemed like several hours—it was only 90 minutes—we pulled into the terminal in Belize City. The bus, completely crammed with sweaty humanity from front to back and top to bottom drained in a flash, as though the roof had burst off and we all came flowing out like a tidal wave. Everyone knew where they were going, except me of course, so they raced to the exits and left me standing there looking around like a lost child. I looked left, then right, then straight ahead, hoping to catch a glimpse of a sign indicating water taxis to Caye Caulker, which I expected I would see rather quickly. I found a sign that looked promising however there was no indication as to where I should go to get tickets.

A taxi driver caught my attention with an outstretched hand. Rather than dismiss him as I am prone to do I engaged him in a quick conversation.

"How much is it to the water taxi terminal?"

He looked me up and down, determining how much he was going to charge me.

"Six Belizean dollars, I mean seven."

Rather than fight him over the equivalent of fifty cents I relented, put my ego aside and said, "Let's go."

"Okay, sir."

I was hot, a bit nauseous from the bus ride, and didn't really care how much it cost. It was only a few dollars after all.

A few minutes later, after dashing through what may have qualified as streets in some countries, and amongst the stench of the "river" (an open sewage ditch) we arrived at the water taxi terminal. I had all of five minutes to spare before the next water taxi left so I bought my there-and-back ticket and sat down. As I scanned the scene I noticed a tour office offering bus services to Flores, Guatemala, my next intended destination. I darted inside and chatted up a young Indian man, who, oddly, was carrying three or four cell phones, and asked him a few questions. As I had come to know from my time in India everything was "possible" with him so I confirmed four or five different ways the details of the bus service, including departure and arrival times and quality of bus. I knew it would not end up being what was promised but at least I felt better after having peppered him with questions.

I jumped on the departing boat at the last minute and settled in for an hour of fun and games bouncing up and down and up and down over what seemed to me to be unnecessarily large and unfriendly waves. My nausea from the bus was amplified by the boat, almost to the point of throwing up. I somehow kept it together, despite the sweat dripping from my forehead and chills running up and down my spine. Everyone else on the boat seemed so perfectly comfortable that it pissed me off.

Upon arrival, at the end of the dock, I was greeted by a sun-grizzled local named Gilbert who inquired, "Do you need accommodation, friend?"

My first reaction was to say no but I decided to just go with it. I was traveling rather freely, after all, so there was no need to be like my usual self.

"I'm looking to go cheap," I said.

"No problem. We have cheap," he replied.

"What have you got? I'm not going to piss around with you."

"There's a nice place at the end of the street, this way," he said as he directed me with an extended hand.

"Is it nice?"

"They have beach access and it's very cheap. Take a look here," he said as he demonstrated his well-worn binder full of aged and awful pictures.

I had a feeling the place was probably pretty nice a couple of decades ago, but not so much anymore. Again, I let it go. It didn't matter how nice it was. All I needed was a place to rest my head. I didn't need a contemporary, high-class, 5-star experience. I had arrived in a ball of sweat, with a cheap t-shirt and shorts clinging to my body while carrying a worn and stained backpack that had traveled several times the distance of the circumference of the planet; why did I need anything fancy?

As we walked down the sand street toward the end of it, where I could see an ugly yellow building, I noticed something unusual on the right-hand side of the street. There stood what looked like a small billboard though it did not have an advertisement on it, it was completely white. As I looked closer I saw a number of chairs on the ground in front of it, positioned in rows. It appeared to be an outdoor movie theater.

"What's that?" I asked Gilbert as we walked past.

"That's a movie theater."

"They actually show movies there? What kind of movies?"

"There is a special showing this week of a Belizean movie. It's the first time there has been a Belizean movie."

"It's showing this week?"

"Yes, for the next couple of nights, I think. You should check it out."

"Maybe I will."

Gilbert, I deduced, did not work for the hotel, but was a freelance worker making a few bucks every time he brought someone from the dock to one of the many cheap stays on the tiny island. He grabbed a key from the front desk and showed me a room. When I saw it I had an immediate flashback to the room I had stayed in Uyuni, Bolivia during my world-trip, which won my unofficial award as the nastiest room of my journey. Sadly, this Caye Caulker representation topped even that. Words could not describe it. I had an involuntary guttural response, a heave really. I held it back and quickly turned to Gilbert.

"Got anything else? I prefer one with its own bathroom."

"Sure, there's another one further back from the beach; maybe a bit more private."

"Sounds great; let's check that one out."

He exchanged keys at the front desk and showed me another room. It was not much better, if at all. The linoleum on the floor was torn to shreds, the two sagging twin beds sported horrible yellow-coloured sheets displaying a rainbow of stains topped by razor-thin pillows. The walls were awash in yellow and pink – causing me to close my eyes until they were almost completely shut, allowing them to get used to the visual noise. Once they adjusted I saw the walls were cracked, the paint peeling, and streaks of brown and red were splashed across them. It was, simply put, a dump. I turned to Gilbert and met his expectant eyes. I knew a few dollars hung in the balance for him. He looked worn, beaten, and almost as fragile as the room in which we stood. Part of me was disgusted, not wanting to stay there and possibly be eaten by nasty bugs in the middle of the night, and another part wanted to just go with it, as I had told myself I would. I just needed to sleep there after all. When I said "I'll take it," a broad smile crossed Gilbert's leathery face.

Caye Caulker was nothing more than a slightly less congested version of San Pedro, and available at a much lower price-point. As I walked one of the few streets the length of the tiny island I thought of my visit to Kho Phi Phi Island in Thailand many years before. It was not as congested and lacked, thankfully, the constantly thumping music that Thais are so fond of. The tempo of Caye Caulker was also slower, and there was nobody asking me every ten seconds if I wanted a taxi boat ride somewhere.

The streets were packed with restaurants and hotels, tightly fit next to one another in a continuous stream, like row houses. Interspersed amongst the restaurants and hotels were tour operators and the occasional grocery store. Many of the buildings were well worn, some almost falling apart. Every couple of blocks there was a for sale sign attached to a small bungalow or store front with accommodation above. The prices on these properties indicated to me that there was still plenty of demand from the U.S. and Europe for investment or vacation properties. I couldn't imagine paying top-dollar for a shack on a tiny island so compact you could hear your neighbours breathe or go to the bathroom.

The grocery stores on the island were all dimly-lit and jammed to the rafters with shelves full of products, most of which were of the snack and junk food variety. In one store the lady behind the counter was so enthralled with the Chinese soap opera she was watching on her laptop that she failed to notice I was standing there for several minutes. When she finally did realize I was there she shot me a look of disdain, bordering on anger, for having interrupted her. She quickly snatched the cash from my hand, threw the change on the counter and went back to her soap opera. She looked back over her shoulder to bark something at her teenaged son (at least I assumed it was her son; otherwise there may have been some child labour law infringement going on) and gave me the "get the hell out of my store" look, shifting her eyes from me to the door and back. I felt like I was intruding, as though I was standing in the middle of their living room. I scooted out as quickly as I could.

As I wandered aimlessly along the few sandy streets of Caye Caulker I felt a sense of calm come over me. My pace slowed to the point I could feel each step as my feet contacted the ground. My heart rate and breathing slowed as well. The moist warm air splashed my face gently as I strode along. The feeling of the air on my skin reminded me of previous times I had spent in tropical climates – times I was often escaping the bitter cold of Canadian winters. Mexico, Cuba, Southeast Asia; the images came to my mind in quick succession. I felt a sense of excitement in my stomach, the feeling of the loosening of muscles and of breaths reaching much deeper into me. A blissful relaxation overtook me. I was moving so slowly I nearly stopped on the spot to take it all in. I had succumbed to the slow pace of the island.

Back at the front desk of my hotel I struggled, again, to get someone's attention. Maybe *I* just wasn't noteworthy? The woman who appeared to be the manager, or owner, finally acknowledged me. A woman in her late forties, she tried desperately, and unsuccessfully, to look much younger. She wore very heavy makeup, especially around the eyes. The bright blue eye shadow glistened with perspiration, making her look downright scary. She wore large hoop earrings and a gaudy ring on each of her chunky fingers. Her fingernails were long enough to spear and kill anything up to the size of a small dog from a distance of a few feet and were painted a rainbow of colours. Her ample mass hung out above and below a blouse that was many, many sizes too small.

"Hi, dear, how can I help you?" she asked.

"I wanted to pay for the snorkeling tour tomorrow," I replied, trying not to look directly at her crooked, stained, and sometimes missing teeth.

"Right." She looked confused.

"I checked in a few hours ago. I'm in room twenty-one. I told you I wanted to take the snorkeling tour. I wanted to pay for that now."

"Right. Yes, of course." She shuffled some papers on the desk.

I thought maybe she was a little distraught by something as she seemed to move in slow motion while she stared off into space.

"What room are you in?"

"Twenty-one," I repeated.

"Right. I'll just put your name down in my book here. What was your name again?"

"Jason."

"Right. Well, okay then. You're set to go. Have a good night," she said as she walked abruptly out of the office.

"Alright," I said, wondering if my name and room number ended up on some random piece of paper or not. I headed back to my room feeing unsure about the whole thing.

I woke up the next morning much earlier than necessary because the room had been just shy of a million degrees all night. The two rickety old ceiling fans that spun overhead had done nothing to cool the room. I had flip-flopped for hours, unable to get back to sleep, mostly concerned about those fans crashing down on my prone body and causing irreparable damage to my private parts. I finally got up, not feeling at all rested. I headed out to Amor Y Café, the only establishment I had noticed the day before that seemed to be a breakfast place. They were open from 6:00am to "midday" whereas other places did not open until "about" 8:00am. I ordered the most expensive thing on the menu, a bowl of yogurt with fruit and granola, and savoured it leisurely.

A Most Improbable Adventure

Later I went to the pier at the hotel to be picked up for the snorkeling tour. A massive black man named Sean with even more massive dreadlocks hanging from the back of his head greeted me. Along with a couple of other people I hopped into a tiny little boat that would take us just a few hundred metres down the shore to the equipment shop where we would meet the rest of the group and get outfitted with masks and fins.

I sat on a picnic table as Sean scrounged through the hut filled with snorkeling gear. A couple, Daniel and Alicia from Uruguay, sat with me. They were getting ready to go to the barrier reef that day. In their early fifties they looked like seasoned travelers. He wore a hat that fastened under the chin while she wore a swimsuit and sunglasses, her skin showing the effects of many, many years under the sun. They had been traveling through Belize, Guatemala and Mexico for several weeks. They owned a country lodge in Uruguay, I learned. Alicia was clearly the marketer of the operation as she went on to tell me all about the place, including the fact that it was a self-sustaining eco-lodge and had been featured on T.V. many times, including on CNN.

"What do you do?" she asked. *Again with that fucking question.*

"I'm in banking," I lied. *I'm actually a rodeo clown, thanks for asking.*

While Alicia and I were chatting her husband simply sat back and observed. In fact, he seemed to be sort of looking off into the distance rather content with just sitting there and feeling the warm breeze blow in off the ocean. He seemed so relaxed and happy. I had the feeling he was the strong, silent type in the relationship and the business operation; the kind of guy that quietly went about things, making sure everything was taken care of. I thought of my father-in law Gerry at that moment. He was exactly that kind of guy. He made sure things got done; sometimes the things nobody else wanted to do, or would even notice. He provided such strength to his wife and family and did it with no fanfare. He told the occasional story but mostly was just the rock of the family and someone I looked up to very much. I identified with Gerry as I thought of myself as that kind of rock for my family as well.

Our guides for the snorkeling tour were Raul and José. Our first stop on the tour was Hol Chan Reserve, where we were met by what amounted to park rangers as they lounged on their boat. José exchanged some paperwork with one of them and we were off to our first site. After being in the water for only about ten minutes I had already seen more sea life than on any other snorkeling tour I had ever been on. Dozens of colourful fish surrounded me, almost as though they were asking me to play with them. José coaxed an eel out of the reef and was able to pet it on the head a few times before it ducked back into its hole.

José, despite being significantly overweight for a man of diminutive stature, moved with a graceful and athletic fluidity in the water. There were no wasted movements as he dove deep to point out things to us. I struggled to keep up with him as he led the pack from one spot to the next. Juan, who was no more than twenty years old and no more than 125 pounds, was like a giant dark-skinned fish. He moved effortlessly and seemed to never come up for air. He would dive deep, turn upside down, roll, spin, and frolic for what seemed like ten minutes before returning to the surface for a quick gulp of air. At one point he spelled his name with his finger on the silt-covered back of a passing manta ray much the way you might write "wash me" on the side of a dirty car.

In Shark Alley, a rather aptly named snorkel and dive site, Juan filled up a conch shell with small, dead fish and then dropped it in the water. The sharks and rays scrambled around the shell, whipping up the sand on the sea floor like a mini tornado, looking for a nice snack. We all kept our distance as we watched the sharks with open mouths devour everything in their path. Everyone except Juan of course. He rather casually

A Most Improbable Adventure

floated right in the middle of the maelstrom and emerged with not a scratch. If fact, he quickly went back to the boat and reloaded the then empty shell with more fish for round two. I could only imagine how well fed those sharks must have been as different tour groups stopped by several times a day.

Not long after we left Shark Alley I started to feel a bit nauseous. The water was rather calm, but by no means still. Despite not quite feeling right I went back in the water to see the manatees, something I had never seen before. I was surprised at how graceful they were as they seemed, despite their massive weight, to hang suspended in the water. As I watched them slowly turn and maneuver around in the water the nausea came back to me, this time more strongly. I decided it was time to get back on the boat. I had had very bad motion sickness in the past and I did not want to chance anything and make it worse. I got back to the boat, dried off, and sat quietly with my head hung and forearms on my legs as I hunched over.

Incredibly, not two minutes later another of the group came aboard suffering the same fate. It was one of the two English ex-soldiers that had been, by their own accounts, out drinking to excess the night before. He was a beefy young man in otherwise great shape but he had been reduced to a sickly child as he began to throw up repeatedly over the back of the boat. Amazingly, this made me feel a little better. I was in much better condition than he was; I didn't feel the need to vomit but my head was woozy. One of the ladies on the boat, Karen, gave us both motion sickness pills and some friendly advice for next time.

"Thanks," I said, as I downed the pills.

"You should feel better in about twenty minutes. I took mine before I came, that's usually the best time to take them," she said.

"Yeah, I usually do but not today. Are you feeling okay?" I asked.

"I have no problem with motion sickness today. My legs are tired though. I have a steel plate in the leg that makes it hard to be active for too long before I get tired."

"A steel plate? Did you have surgery?"

"Actually I was shot a few years ago. The bullet shattered my femur."

"Wow, you were shot? How did that happen?"

"I was a federal officer in Louisiana. I exchanged fire with someone and I got the worst of it. I ended up having to retire because I couldn't go back to work after that. Like I said, I can still do things but my leg gets tired pretty quickly."

I didn't feel like pushing the questioning any further, though I did want to know the details of what happened. It was clear she was done talking about it and I didn't want to re-hash her trauma. I tried to transition the conversation on a positive note.

"Well, it's amazing that you are able to do this at all. Really, it's quite something," I said.

She gave me a polite smile, acknowledging the end of the conversation.

As the boat docked at the end of the tour one of the other ladies struck up a conversation with me. Her name was Nancy. She was from Chicago and was only three weeks into a year-long sabbatical from being a school vice principal. After years and years of teaching and working in administration she decided she would do a round-the-world trip. Of course I was immediately intrigued, having had a round-the-world adventure myself, and we chatted as we got out of the boat and walked up the pier to the beach. We then dropped off our snorkeling equipment at the guide's shop. We decided to keep walking and talking; neither of us had anywhere to be after all.

After strolling rather aimlessly we decided it was time for ice cream and promptly found a place to have some and sat down to continue our discussion. Her trip had only just begun so she was full of excitement and energy about what she was doing and about to do. She was living the *Eat, Pray, Love* dream and many of her friends could not understand why.

"They said 'Are you having a mid-life crisis or something?'" she said.

"I got a lot of questions when I told people I was doing a round-the-world trip, too," I chuckled. "I know exactly what you're talking about."

"Eventually they understood that I just wanted to do this. I didn't need any more of an explanation than that," she continued.

"That's fantastic. Good for you."

"I know I won't regret it," she beamed.

"You absolutely will not regret it. That's so great. Did you notice that once you decided to do it everything else just fell into place?"

"Yes, it did. It all worked out. There are still lots of things I haven't planned yet but that's okay. I like it that way. I know the rest will continue to work out just fine."

Before I knew it about an hour had passed. I wanted to head back to my room for some rest. "What are you doing with the rest of your day?" I asked.

"I was going to go to that movie theater tonight. Apparently there is a Belizean movie showing. It's supposed to be a big deal. Do you want to go see it?" she asked.

"I heard about that, too. The guy that brought me to the hotel I'm staying at told me about the movie. It's not much of a theater but how often do you get a chance to see a Belizean movie? Sure, let's go."

The movie was called *The Legend of Xtabai* (pronounced ish-tab-eye, more or less). It was the Caye Caulker premier and there was a red-carpet feel to the tiny outdoor theater – with a bar and everything. Nancy ordered a cocktail and we took two seats (there were only about twenty to choose from) dead-centre. I had no idea what I was about to witness. Within minutes a man appeared at the front and began to speak. What struck me about him was that he was clearly not Belizean.

"Good evening everyone and thanks for coming," he said. "My name is Matt and I am the director of the movie you are about to watch. I just wanted to say thanks for being here tonight for this Caye Caulker premier. This movie was first seen not long ago at the Belizean Film Festival and it is the only full-length feature film ever shot and produced here in Belize. We are very excited about it and we hope that you enjoy it. I will be available after the movie, along with a couple of the actors, for a question and answer period. Please sit back and enjoy the show."

I turned to Nancy with what must have been a look of complete confusion. I was trying to comprehend what was going on. It was a Belizean movie directed by a small white man and the movie had recently premiered at the *Belizean* Film Festival.

"There's a Belizean Film Festival, apparently," I said.

"Apparently so," she replied, looking as confused as I likely did.

Neither of us had a clue what the movie was about and before we could reconcile what was going on the movie started.

My mother once told me that if you can't say anything nice you shouldn't say anything at all, so I didn't. At the end of the movie the director got up again and took questions. The first few questions from the audience were not questions at all – they were accolades for having produced some sort of masterpiece. The audience absolutely loved it and many people were literally bursting with pride. During the question and answer I learned two things that helped explain the quality of the film: there was no script and nobody in the film had acted before.

Matt, the director, had gone on to tell us that the film was originally supposed to be a much shorter documentary but after only a few days they decided to make it a feature, which required more actors. They recruited people randomly off the street after a casting call attracted absolutely nobody. A casting call, it would appear, in a country where a feature film

A Most Improbable Adventure

has never been made, had absolutely no meaning to anyone. They therefore picked people off the streets and asked if they would like to be in a movie. What 20-year-old girl in Belize wouldn't want to be in a movie? The best "actor" in the film, in my estimation, was actually one of the producers.

Each scene was completely improvised, he went on to say. There was no script to work from so they just went with it and then fine-tuned in the event of a re-take. This much was clear to me when watching the movie as many scenes were simply confusing with too many people talking at the same time.

Matt said that he shot the movie in only eight days. He said that since it had never been done before there was no model to follow so he just winged it. Much of the footage was shot in the jungle, away from anything that might slow them down. The few scenes shot in urban settings went quickly also as there were no permits to obtain in order to do so. It may have helped that a couple of scenes had the actual Belizean Army in them.

The whole experience was just too bizarre. Trying to figure out how I ended up at a Belizean movie in Caye Caulker was just too much for my brain to process. It got more complex when I approached Matt after the question and answer period. He was rather short but had a huge smile and infectious energy. He wore shorts and a tank top, as anyone should on a typically warm Caye Caulker evening. He looked relaxed with a cocktail in his hand.

"Where are you from, Matt?" I asked.

"I'm originally from Ottawa, Canada, but I'd been living in L.A. for the past four years," he replied.

"A Canadian! That's great. I'm from Calgary but have been living in Toronto for the past ten years."

"We Canadians seem to be everywhere!" he said as he smiled.

"That's for sure. Tell me, how did this movie come about?"

"I arrived in Belize almost a year ago," he started. "It was my intention to spend four months traveling through Central

America on my way to Panama. I completely stumbled into this and haven't left yet," he laughed.

"It's funny how these things work out," I offered.

"I know. One day I saw some people on the street struggling to use some film cameras and other equipment. It looked like they needed some assistance. Since I'm a filmmaker it kind of made sense that I help out. Before long I was basically training them on how to use the equipment and the basics of shooting and editing. That sort of morphed into a project, which morphed into a movie. It all happened incredibly fast. It went from concept to release in three months. This kind of thing can't happen in the U.S. or Canada. It would have taken forever with the red tape."

"That's incredible."

"I know. It's crazy. We had no script, no experienced actors, nothing. We just sort of went with it and the next thing you know we have a movie."

"Did you literally just talk to people on the street to get them to try out?"

"We sure did. A casting call doesn't mean anything here. We had to go out on the street and meet people. It was really something."

"I'll say. This whole story is really quite incredible. It seems the folks here are very excited about this movie."

"I know. The locals have been this way from the beginning. They are so proud."

"Well, congratulations. You really made something out of nothing here. That's awesome. Best of luck to you."

"Thanks so much."

With that we parted ways. I started to ponder how a Canadian filmmaker, traveling through Central America for a few months, happened to stumble on a bunch of people struggling to make a documentary—it all seemed so normal, didn't it? And there I was, just talking to the filmmaker after having seen his movie in a tiny outdoor theater on a tiny island just off the coast of a small Central American country and doing so with a school vice principal from Chicago on sabbatical and in the very early stages of a round the world trip. Yes, indeed, it was all very normal.

Again I had come across a very unusual story of someone who had created a life out of something unpredictable. Matt was only planning on traveling for a few months and a life of greater fulfillment seemed to find him. Whether he consciously sought it out, I didn't know, but I saw before me a man full of light and energy and someone who looked like he was in his element. He surely felt what I was thinking: if you can make a movie from seemingly nothing in Belize you can do almost anything. I wondered where he might end up next.

After our theatrical experience Nancy and I went about searching for food, as neither of us had eaten since our ice cream treat much earlier that afternoon. It was getting late so our options were limited, especially given that it was low season and many restaurants were simply closed for the season. Luckily we found someone willing to serve us at that hour and we dined on lobster and rice. We talked for a few more hours about travel and our lives back in our respective realities. We parted ways with a "good luck" not knowing if we might run into each other again in Central America somewhere.

I awoke late the next day as I couldn't hear my watch alarm due to the whizzing noise of the two ceiling fans set on high speed all night. I had just enough time to have a quick shower, gather my stuff, and walk to the pier before the boat arrived for the trip back to Belize City. Fortunately the ride back was not as choppy as the ride there so I was not as nauseas as I had been before. I was happy to arrive, however, and get on with the next leg of my journey – to Flores, Guatemala. I purchased a seat from the gentleman at the tourist office and was set to go. All I had to do was wait.

As I stood there I overheard three young men with backpacks talking about their Caye Caulker experience – mostly tales of drinking too much. A passerby approached them and asked where they were from. "Vancouver, Canada," they replied, in almost perfect unison. Normally I would be interested in speaking with my fellow Canadians but I had no such desire to speak to them at that moment.

As I stood waiting for the bus to Flores a man startled me from behind, "Can I ask you a question?" I turned to see a slight man of perhaps fifty or so, eyes drooping, sweating profusely and struggling to stand. He seemed rather intoxicated. He looked European but with a very deep tan.

"What can I help you with?" I replied. He then mumbled something I couldn't quite make out. "I'm sorry, I don't understand," I said.

"Sure you do. I'm speaking English too," he slurred.

"Sorry, I just didn't hear you before."

"I'm going to Caye Caulker," he said as he nearly fell over. "I seem to have lost my wallet in the celebrations."

"What celebrations?"

"It's our independence this month."

"I see. And you lost your wallet?"

"I know what you're thinking and I'm not one of those…"

"One of those what?"

"I seem to have lost my wallet and I need to get to Caye Caulker," he said, seemingly unaware of the incomplete sentence he had left hanging a moment before.

"I think I have a couple of bucks," I said as I reached into my pocket where I knew I had some coins. I pulled out two Belizean dollar coins and put them in his shaking hand.

"I need to get to Caye Caulker, he repeated. Again oblivious to what had just happened.

"Yes, I know. You told me. I just gave you two dollars. You can go to that office right over there to get a ticket," I said as I pointed to the ticket office not far away. I wanted to get rid of this guy as I wanted no part of the conversation, such as it was, any longer.

"Okay, then, have a great trip," I said.

"Well, what's that?" he said.

"What are you talking about?" I said as I set my hands on my hips, about ready to walk away from the insanity. He then mimicked me, putting his hands on his hips. He thrust his chest out in some feeble attempt to establish a manly presence. That was it—I lost it.

"Look, you don't have to be such an ass," I barked. "I gave you a couple of bucks so you should be on your way." My voice and my temperature were rising. There was only one thing worse than an obnoxious drunk and that was an ungrateful obnoxious drunk.

His eyes opened wide. I looked directly into them, pursing my lips and stiffening my jaw. What was this idiot going to do?

"I guess you're one of those," he said.

"One of what?" I nearly yelled. "Get the fuck out of my face and get on your boat," I said as I waved my arm toward the ticket booth again. I stepped back so as to give him space to either do something even more stupid or do the smart thing and bugger off. He only stared at me, trying to think of what to do or say.

"Go!" I blasted, not giving him the chance to say anything. His gaze fell to my feet and he turned, ever so slowly, to walk away. As he did I wondered if he actually did lose his wallet. I doubted it but after that ridiculous demonstration I hoped against hope.

I watched as he stumbled over and sat down quietly between two women waiting for the next boat. He turned to say something to the younger one. She immediately put up her hand as if to say no and went back to texting on her phone. I continued to watch. Minutes passed and he just sat there, struggling mightily to stay upright. He then turned to a woman sitting on the bench behind him. They spoke briefly. She then reached into her purse and gave him something. He nodded to her and turned back around. Several more minutes passed and then he stood to go to the ticket office. He milled about in the office for another few minutes so as to complete the masquerade and then casually left the office and made his way to the exit of the pier, past a couple of restaurants and shops. Ever so casually he slipped out the exit – a few bucks richer. I had encountered my trip's first idiot, only a few days in.

The bus bound for Flores arrived right on time—if on time means an hour and a half late. It was, of course, of a lower quality than was promised. The pictures of what I thought I was going to get were of large, modern, sturdy, air conditioned buses with smiling drivers wearing crisp, white, collared shirts. What showed up was an aged rattle trap on bald tires with no air conditioning or padding left on the bench seats. Naturally I was pissed off but I didn't say anything and just got in. By my normal standards this particular rust bucket was a decrepit hunk of decayed metal and offered no more than a fifty-fifty chance of getting me to where I wanted to go. However, I was not in Toronto, I was in Central America. I had to remind myself of that every once in a while. I was excited to get to Guatemala and focused on that rather than the rough ride I knew I was in for.

EL FUEGO AWAKENS

I sweat like a stuck pig for the entire five-hour ride to Flores. The border crossing into Guatemala was relatively straightforward. The most difficult part of it all was fighting my way through the mob of money changers that stormed the bus when it stopped, flashing enormous wads of bills in their hands. I thought back briefly to my currency exchange experience in the airport in Mexico City and thought I'd better avoid these shady characters. After slipping through their clutches I made my way to the line-up to enter Guatemala. For only a few dollars I was granted access for ninety days.

Upon arrival in Santa Elena, the mainland sister city to Flores, we were told to get out of the bus and get into a shuttle van. No explanation was given, we were just dumped off and the bus drove away. Eventually a shuttle van showed up. The driver told us that big buses could not drive on the compact streets of Flores so we had to take their shuttle. That made me feel better. At least we weren't being taken captive.

I ended up in a shuttle with the loud boys from Vancouver, two young guys from Australia who looked the part of the haggard long-term travelers they likely were and an Argentinian guy who looked like he stepped off a magazine cover and into the van. We later stopped at what the driver promised us was "the only cash machine open today" and pocketed some

Quetzales. We were then swept away to a tour office where hotels and tours were forced on us. Again, I went with it.

My reason for going to Flores was because it is the main jump off point for visiting Tikal—one of the ancient Mayan world's most revered sites and one of my bucket list items—so I was glad to make plans to go there with the pleasant young lady behind the desk. I also wanted to go to Antigua so I made those plans too. I then chose the second hotel room they showed to me. It was nothing spectacular of course but at least it had air conditioning. I was set up with accommodations and activities for the next few days and had only been in Flores for ten minutes. A strange sense of accomplishment came over me.

I dropped my backpack down on the single bed in my one-star hotel room and headed out to orient myself on the small island of Flores. I failed. Flores is like Venice – small, compact, and full of alleyways and unmarked streets. I did find an Internet café so I could touch base with Isabelle via email and I then headed out for dinner. Slow season again was to my benefit as I easily found a seat at a nearly deserted restaurant.

Despite not having had anything other than junk food to eat for nearly a day I was not particularly hungry. The heat had killed my appetite but I knew I needed to eat some protein to keep my energy up. I had two extremely small chicken fajitas and headed back to my room and turned in early. I needed to be up at 4:00am for the trip to Tikal and I drifted off quickly once my head hit the pillow.

Despite falling asleep quickly I was not able to stay asleep long. The bed sagged badly in the middle so I was surrounded by foul-smelling mattress no matter where I positioned myself. I tossed and turned all night, keeping an eye on my watch alarm; not wanting to oversleep. Suddenly the T.V. turned on. It was 4:00am. *What the hell was that?* The blaring T.V. startled me but once I got my bearings and remembered where I was I turned the T.V. off and started to think again.

A Most Improbable Adventure

Maybe the hotel knew that I was going to Tikal that morning and needed to be up early so the T.V. was set to turn on as an alarm? Regardless, I was up and ready to go and standing in front of the hotel at 4:30am as instructed. As the minutes passed while I stood there I joked to myself how 4:30am my time was about 5:00am Guatemala time. Nothing ever actually happened on time, right?

As I continued to wait in the dark the guard from the hotel—or the random guy that slept on the couch by the front door—peeked outside and whispered something to me. I couldn't hear him, let alone understand him, so I asked him to repeat. Suddenly he disappeared and a moment later reappeared with a sitting stool in his hand. He put it down on the sidewalk in front of the hotel and I gladly sat down to rest. Coming down the road I saw what looked like a tourist van, its lights glowing in the darkness. The van stopped a couple of houses short of the hotel. It was, in fact, a police truck. Not a minute later a police officer appeared in the distance walking with a man who appeared to be in handcuffs. He tossed the man in the back of the truck and sped off down the dead-quiet street. What did he do, I thought? I hadn't heard that Flores was a dangerous place, but maybe it was. Suddenly I felt a little unsafe, sitting out there in the dark all by myself.

I continued to pace back and forth on the sidewalk in front of the hotel for another half-hour before a shuttle bus appeared. A man jumped out of the passenger-side door before the bus came to a stop and asked for my ticket. I showed it to him, which he then looked over very carefully for what seemed like several minutes, and then he said "Wrong company. They are coming later." Suddenly a woman appeared in the doorway of my hotel, looking disheveled and somewhat panicked. She rushed past me and showed the man her ticket and hopped in. I settled back onto my rickety stool.

Another forty minutes passed before the shuttle bus showed up. I tried not to be pissed off about getting up so early only to stand outside for what seemed like forever. The shuttle was old and beaten up, and, of course, completely jammed with sweating humanity. I struggled through everyone in an attempt to reach the last seat in the back row. The faces I passed looked very tired, possibly even slightly annoyed. Within a minute we were off the island and into Santa Elena. Another brief moment passed before we stopped at another hotel to pick up more passengers. In hopped the three loud kids from Vancouver—they were inescapable.

Upon arrival at the gate to the site the smiling face of our guide, Luis, popped his head in through the now open door of the van. He was to be the guide at Tikal for English-speakers. Our group consisted of the aforementioned boys from Vancouver, a German named George, two girls from England, a guy from Japan (who I suspected did not really understand much English) and six young girls from Israel who loved to chat, excessively. I thought it might be Lamanai all over again—too many people talking and not enough paying attention. What there was not, thankfully, was a wife berating her husband over absolutely everything.

"I grew up around this area," Luis offered. "My parents worked here for decades. I used to sell drinks to tourists when I was as young as seven. I know this place very well."

Luis was perhaps forty, nearly bald and slightly pudgy in the face. He wore brown work boots, brown cargo pants, and a black DC United soccer shirt. It made me sweat just looking at him. He had great energy and pointed out absolutely everything he saw, including a tarantula that he coaxed out of a hole and held close to his mouth as if to take a bite.

One of the men in the group, George, tall and handsome with a square jaw and perfect teeth, was, I learned, living in Guatemala City as a part of a school internship. He couldn't speak Spanish before arriving in Guatemala but was able to carry a conversation with Luis quite well, in my estimation.

A Most Improbable Adventure

"I've been here almost three months but I'll be going back to Germany soon," he said.

"Your English is great. Where did you learn it?" I asked.

"I did two years of high school and then two years of college in the U.S., in North Carolina."

"Wow, that's pretty cool. You speak German, English, and Spanish. Are there any other languages you speak?

"No, that's it," he said, looking legitimately disappointed that he spoke only three languages.

He was working for Starbucks, buying fair trade beans in Guatemala. His school had internships all over the world and in order to graduate students had to do several of them overseas. Here was a young man working in the middle of nowhere, a decidedly more dangerous place than his own country, learning a new language, and all in the name of higher education. I was impressed.

It also stirred up in me the regret of having never done anything similar during my days at university. This perfectly nice young man made me mad at myself (okay, I was a little jealous of him too) for not doing more interesting things when I was younger. I remembered seeing postings on the walls of the business school at the University of Calgary offering various credit-gathering opportunities to study abroad. I always talked myself out of even truly considering these things. Why? Was it really too expensive or was it simply just too scary? The age-old saying is true: it's the things we *don't* do that we regret.

George then gave me some advice about Guatemala.

"Don't go to Guatemala City. There is nothing there. No history, no architecture, and nothing to do."

"Really? I thought I would spend a day or two there just checking it out, exploring."

"If you have the time then maybe. If you don't there are plenty of other places to go for sure. Panajachel, Antigua, Lake Atitlán, Semuc Champey."

"I was planning to go to at least some of those places anyway, but it's good to hear from someone who has been living in the country and has explored these places. Thanks." He changed my mind right away about Guatemala City – it was going to be a transition city for me anyway but with limited time I really could skip it for greener pastures.

We proceeded to talk for the next hour or so as we walked amongst the ruins of Tikal, he sharing the travel experiences of his young life and I sharing some of the experiences of my world trip and the writing of my first book. Each question he asked drove my mind back into the archives to retrieve the images and feelings of my journey. I felt like I was being interviewed by a reporter. I relived the adventure, and the feelings it elicited in me, with each story I recounted. He was genuinely interested in my stories and I could tell he was taking mental notes. I also felt something else – pride. I felt important somehow. For those brief few moments I felt like I was a rock star being asked by an adoring fan for an autograph. It was odd, uncomfortable, and ego-expanding all at the same time.

Later, I stood in the Great Plaza where I felt like I was at the centre of a large soccer pitch. The two pyramids in the plaza, Templo 1 at 47-metres high and Templo 2 at 38-metres, stand opposite one another, like massive goalies defending their respective ends of the pitch. The Central Acropolis and North Acropolis that border the plaza were like the stands where the crazed fans would sit. Despite the expansive space it somehow felt very intimate. Due to the placement of the buildings the acoustics were such that I was able to hear people talking in far-off conversations throughout the plaza.

After a somewhat perilous climb I sat atop Templo 4 gazing out over the jungle of Tikal. For as far as I could see there was a deep green canopy that formed an elevated carpet that I could almost reach out and touch. The hills in the distance were just as deeply coloured as the canopy right below me. Templo 4 is the tallest structure at Tikal and at 70-metres high is one of the tallest in the Mayan world. I tried with great difficulty to ignore the incessant chatting of the Israeli girls and Canadian boys and tried to focus on my breathing and my mantra. My eyes closed, my breathing slowed, and I sat motionless as the hot sun drenched my face and arms. Sweat began to drip down my back, chest, and forehead. I focused on my mantra and faded out for just a few moments of peace and quiet. The breeze was light but much needed and much appreciated. I felt as though I could slip off the edge of the platform and fly away over the jungle to Templo 1 and Templo 2, two of few visible structures above the canopy. Just as quickly as I faded away I came back to the present moment to the cackling laughter of the Canadian boys reverberating off the stone behind me. *Damn, I was having a good moment there.*

As the tour went on the Israeli girls talked more and more and more. *What could they possibly be talking about?* The more they talked the more they got bitten by a vast selection of bugs and ants. It was sweet justice. They eventually gave up, packed it in, and went back to the restaurant at the entrance to the site. It perplexed me as I considered how anyone could travel such a vast distance and pay real money to see the wonders of Tikal and then just leave because of a few bugs.

When the guide-led part of the tour was over Luis gave us instructions on how to get to various other parts of the site we hadn't seen yet. I decided to go to the area of the site that was the absolute farthest away from everything else – Templo 6. I hoped that none of the chatty people would go there so I could get a few minutes of quiet. As luck would have it I was completely alone. I had walked for several minutes in what I had hoped was the right direction and then a thought hit me. When was the last time someone was killed by a jaguar on one of these trails? It would be just my luck to come face-to-face with a jaguar now given that I had searched for one while in Africa on my around-the-world trip and came up empty.

Isabelle had told me her only concern about me going on this trip was that I be safe and smart. Was it not smart to be walking on this path completely alone? Perhaps. I could twist an ankle and not make it back in time for my bus, possibly getting stuck in the jungle for days as one poor soul had a few years prior, according to Luis. As I pondered the notion of death by jaguar I felt a tickling sensation on my leg. I looked down to see a number of ants crawling up my shin. As I looked more closely I could see that there were hundreds of them on my shoes. I looked forward, up the path, and saw that the path itself seemed to be moving. There must have been millions of them; the same ants that had been biting everyone in my tour group all day. As far up the path as I could see it was entirely covered.

I was completely surrounded. I let out an audible "fuck" and began to run straight ahead. There was nowhere to go but through them and I didn't have time to plan a more strategic route as they rapidly climbed up my feet and legs. I whacked at them repeatedly as I ran, doing both rather ineffectively. I must have looked like a crazed maniac out there pumping my legs and swatting at the ants at the same time. I felt a tickling sensation on my upper thigh, up under my shorts. Then I really started to run. My backpack slapped against my back, my camera flew about over my shoulder. There seemed no end to the sea of ants. The more I ran the more I seemed to be standing still. Great, I thought, I'm going to twist an ankle, fall and knock myself unconscious on a rock, then the ants will start eating my flesh, *then* the jaguar will come and finish me off.

As I looked up ahead I saw a spot on the path that didn't seem to be moving. A few more wild steps and slaps and I was free. I stood for at least two minutes dancing – prancing really – and smacking my legs, knees, calves, and ankles. Dozens of victims fell off me yet many persisted. Finally, after beating myself nearly senseless, I seemed to subdue the predators

A Most Improbable Adventure

and flicked off the remaining soldiers. I tried to regain my composure and started walking at a brisk pace so as to stay ahead of the now incited horde. I looked down as much as I looked up as I walked. About ten minutes later I saw a sign for Templo 6. A sense of relief washed over me as I had finally received confirmation that I was, indeed, walking in the right direction.

As I rounded a corner I saw the now familiar half-buried structure atop a mound of rubble, dirt, and bush. I slowed for a moment to ponder it. As I stood there I felt the tickling of ants on my legs and was surprised to see that there actually weren't any. After having walked all that way Templo 6 was not much to look at. Mesh screens encased what had been the entrance to the upper temple and graffiti covered it like a blanket, reducing it to nothing more than a derelict inner-city building. I snapped a couple of pictures and went on my way.

As I approached the turnoff to exit the site my eye caught a glimpse of what looked like a very bright lime-green garden hose, upright on the path. It wasn't a garden hose of course, it was a snake. The question was whether it was a vicious and poisonous snake or not. It sensed me and turned in my direction. We had a brief stare down before it dropped and began to slither into the underbrush. It was about four feet long and moved incredibly fast. I stood still and quickly scanned around looking for any of his friends. There appeared to be none so I briskly walked ahead and got back onto the trail. Ants, snakes, and phantom jaguars – that was enough for one day. I made my way to the exit, blowing past the gift shops and scale models of Tikal.

By the time everyone had gathered back at the restaurant a light rain had begun to fall. Moments later it was pouring, hard. Enormous rain drops started hitting the ground as though a bathtub had sprung a massive leak above our heads. Then, sheets of water came down. We all quickly jumped into the shuttle and slammed the door. Our driver cautiously moved forward as the rain pounded into the windshield. The wipers had absolutely no effect as the water continued to pour down. The humidity in the van, already high, shot through the roof. It was a literal sauna – a fully-clothed, disgusting sauna.

For the next hour and a half the driver proceeded in almost complete darkness. Lightning cracked, thunder rumbled, and rain continued to fall. Amazingly, we made it back to Flores without incident, save the flat tire the driver tried to get fixed at three different gas stations before finding someone who actually knew how to do it.

That afternoon I went to an Internet café and used Skype to call Isabelle and the boys. The first connection worked and I saw my family for the first time since I had left home. Isabelle smiled and I smiled back. Sam then appeared in the screen and he jumped up and down with delight, squealing "Daddy, Daddy, Daddy!" My heart almost burst. Tears started to well up in the corners of my eyes. Isabelle then picked up Will, just eight months old, and sat him on her lap. He looked at the screen seeming rather confused. I said, "Hello Sweet Pea. It's Daddy." A huge smile broke out over his face. My heart nearly burst again. My family was all there in that tiny little screen and I was as happy as I could be. After two hours, and a dozen dropped connections, we hung up. It was so good to see my wife and boys. It gave me a quick burst of energy while at the same time I felt very much alone.

I went across the street for a bite of dinner. As I walked into the nearly empty restaurant I noticed the English girls from the Tikal tour. They smiled as they saw me so I walked over. I asked if I could join them and they agreed. Over the next two hours Diane, Emma, and I talked about our current trips, past travel, and places we'd like to go. They were going to Caye Caulker the next day. I was going to Antigua, the place they had most recently come from.

I learned several new English words over the course of our dinner and discussion, including "shiv" (white trash) and "yob"

A Most Improbable Adventure

(young hooligan). We discussed the monarchy, British rule overseas, the American dialect, whether or not Wales is actually a country, and many other delightful topics. It was thoroughly entertaining and a great way to keep my mind off the fact that I missed my family very much.

I awoke abruptly the next morning at 4:00am when the T.V. suddenly turned on, just as it had the morning before. My theory about the hotel knowing I needed to get up was evidently unfounded. For some rather obscure reason the T.V. simply wanted to turn on at that ungodly hour.

I couldn't get back to sleep. A terrible thought entered my mind. Did I put Teddy Bear back in my bag after my Skype call last night? I'd been carrying Sam's little brown teddy bear stuffed animal with me the entire trip, taking pictures of him at important sites and having others take pictures of me with him – all for Sam's benefit. I brought him out during the call to show Sam and he loved it. I know I put Teddy down beside the computer and made a mental note to pick him up before I left.

I got up from bed and turned the light on. I searched everywhere for Teddy. As I did I slowly came to the realization that I had lost him. I felt sick to my stomach. I imagined Sam's little face in the grimace of disappointment. My heart sank. I felt like an ass. I had just let my three-year-old son down in a big way. I had traveled through twenty countries over 155 days carrying my niece's little brown monkey stuffed animal on my world trip without incident and here I had lost my son's teddy bear in only ten days. I struggled mightily to get back to sleep. I tossed and turned for a couple of hours then finally got up.

My bus did not leave until that evening so I simply headed out to see what I could see. I made a stop at the Internet café to check for Teddy—no luck. As I walked past a small trinket shop I made eye contact with a sweet little girl of perhaps four who sat on a small chair outside the shop. Her beautiful face was lit up by an electric smile and bright brown eyes as she sat on her chair, watching people go by with a child's inquisitiveness. As

I approached her our eyes met and I could not look away. Just as I reached her she uttered a tiny "Hola" and raised her hand and waved it ever so slightly. My face broke out in what must have seemed a rather enormous smile. I gently said "Hola" and waved as I passed. It made my day to connect with her like that. I thought immediately of Sam and Will and how much I missed them. I hadn't realized how important that connection with my children was because I had it every day and didn't really think much of it. In the absence of being able to hold and kiss my boys I'd been lacking that physical and emotional connection. That beautiful little girl allowed me to tap into that feeling if only for a brief, fleeting, moment.

As I sat at Cool Beans, perhaps the hippest restaurant on the island (that I could find, anyway) I watched the Guatemalan world go by. Just a few feet from the road, and thus from the water, I watched for hours as people walked by, drove by, or bounced by in the ubiquitous 3-wheel auto rickshaw, which was perfectly suited to the extremely narrow streets of the island. Scooters and motorcycles often had four or more people crowded on. It reminded me of India, where entire families of six or more somehow balanced on motorbikes as they ripped past going entirely too fast. Everyone seemed to be smiling and enjoying life. I was content just sipping my coffee and taking in the breezes off the water.

Before long I found myself on a bus bound for Antigua. As it bounced and swayed I suddenly felt a drop of water on my left arm, the one closest to the window. The rain outside was pounding the bus and now it seemed the rain was creeping in just to make my already difficult sleep even more of a challenge. I pulled back the curtain and was drenched with even more water. It was pitch black outside and inside the bus so I reached for the reading light above my head. Of course it didn't work, and neither did the other button above my neighbour's head. The bus swerved and the curtain swung away from the window and toward me, launching even more water onto my arm, shoulder, and leg. My hands reached out, scrambling in the dark, to find the fastener on the bus wall to which one would normally attach that type of curtain. *Shit, no fastener.* The rain poured and poured, splashing me and flowing onto the floor, where it soaked the bottom of my backpack. As I continued to get soaked the bus swerved and swung and bounced and shook all over the road, inciting the motion sickness that I so dreaded. I dug into my pack and fumbled for several minutes to get my Gravol and popped one into my mouth. It was only two hours into a nine-hour slog from Flores to Antigua and I was wet, motion sick, and extremely tired.

I struggled mightily to avoid touching the dripping wet curtain while arranging the tiny neck and head pillows I had brought along. I flipped from side to side a hundred times if I did it once. The guy next to me seemed to be soundly asleep and clearly he was not getting wet from the rain.

Later, a flash of light startled me awake. I must have drifted off and was jolted back into reality when the intense interior lights of the bus were switched on. We were at some kind of stop along the route, though I had no idea where. The guy who had been beside me had disappeared, as if into thin air. I hoped nobody would take his place. Not a second after I thought it the bus attendant asked the man in the row in front of me to move back to take the vacated seat beside me. A young couple then appeared at the top of the stairs of the upper cabin in which I sat and took their places in the row in front of me. They looked all happy and in love; making my plight seem even worse.

Unfortunately I had neglected to bring my long-sleeved shirt and long pants with me on the bus; two things that would have come in rather handy. I brought everything else except the two items that would have actually helped me in the moment. As I looked around I noticed all the other passengers appropriately attired with sweatshirts and long pants, all snuggled into their seats and snoozing comfortably. In the absence of an appropriate shirt, while the air conditioning continued to blast, I had to pull my arms in through the short-sleeves of my t-shirt and up against my chest so as not to freeze any further.

I flipped and turned and bounced for hours on end and then rather abruptly I awoke to the honking of cars and barking and yelling of men. Just then the bus attendant sprang up the stairs and darted over toward the young tourist couple that sat in the same row as mine but across the aisle. He slapped the man on the knee and began to scream "Rápido! Rápido!" as he waved his arms to indicate we had arrived in Guatemala City and it was time to get the hell off the bus. We all filed off the bus and onto the sidewalk. The bus, it seemed, had simply stopped on the street and thus the dozens of cars and motorbikes behind us had nowhere to go – hence the relentless honking and screaming. The so-called bus station only had room for about four buses to pull in correctly and therefore we had to block the street and get out "Rápido!" The bus jolted away a fraction of a second after the last bag was tossed on the ground, releasing the backed-up traffic as if shot from a cannon, smoke billowing into the already thick and heavy air.

I turned to see a dilapidated terminal building crawling with hawkers and taxi drivers. Several men yelled "Taxi! Taxi!" directly in my face even though I stood only a foot or two away. "No, gracias," I responded each time, avoiding eye contact and shuffling ahead, out of the mayhem. I didn't know what I was looking for but I was told there would be a shuttle there to pick me up and take me on to Antigua. As I scanned around I saw nothing that looked like a shuttle, in fact nothing that looked road-worthy. The young couple I saw on the bus, along with another couple they appeared to be traveling with, jumped into a taxi. I thought briefly that I should do the same. I had little confidence the shuttle would show up and I didn't want to stand around the bus station a second longer than necessary.

A Most Improbable Adventure

Standing near the entrance to the station I saw what looked like the only other tourists from the bus. Two looked European and one Japanese, the latter sporting a very bright yellow jacket—there was no need for a jacket in the hot, sticky weather—emblazoned with Toyota across the back. He looked even more lost than I likely did. I approached one of the Europeans and asked "Do you speak English?"

He slowly and carefully withdrew his mostly smoked cigarette from his lips. He turned to me, seemingly annoyed by my most offensive intrusion. "Yes," he replied, flatly.

"Do you know if there is a shuttle to Antigua leaving from here?"

"Yes," he replied simply, again with a look of annoyance on his face.

"Great, thanks," I offered, in the most cheery voice I could muster under the circumstances. I awaited a reply of some kind; a word, grunt, motion, utterance of any kind but, alas, there was none. I turned and walked away.

Thirty minutes later a shuttle van pulled up and a very dark man jumped out and shouted "Antigua! Antigua! Antigua!" I took this to be the shuttle I was waiting for and immediately rushed for the open door, as did the Europeans and Japanese man, with my ticket extended. I couldn't wait to get on with the rest of the trip. Nobody said a word for the next hour and a half as we made our way through the exhaust-filled streets of Guatemala City and on to Antigua.

Antigua's streets are paved—and I use the word loosely—with stones, none of which were smooth nor properly put in place. This made for an extremely bumpy ride. It was so bad I had to hunch down in my seat so as not to smack my head on the roof of the van.

We were eventually dumped out and given a small map of town and sent on our way. As it was still early in the morning things were rather quiet.

"Do you know where you are going?" I asked the Japanese man.

"I go to *Praza*," he said.

I took this to mean Plaza Mayor, the central town plaza.

"I'm going there too," I said. "Let's head this way," rather guessing that it was the correct direction. I needed to have a central point of reference on the terrible map I was given and what better point of reference than the town plaza?

"Okay," he replied.

We walked in silence for several minutes before the plaza appeared, slowly materializing as if in a dream. The Japanese man then darted off and away, saying nothing, leaving me standing there alone. Before attempting to get my bearings with the map I looked around for a place to get a bite of breakfast and sit down for a minute. I spotted a modern and trendy looking coffee shop whose floor-to-ceiling wall was open to the plaza and headed straight for it. If ever I needed a coffee it was at that moment.

I eagerly devoured a breakfast of granola and yogurt and slowly savoured possibly the best café mocha I had tasted in my life. The caffeine hit me immediately and I was very quickly buzzing. I paid my bill and headed for a hostel I had noted in the travel guide I carried. I hadn't made a reservation but I figured I'd have no problem getting a room. As it turned out, I was wrong. Fortunately they had a sister hostel just around the corner, which is where I was directed. Luckily that place had a private room available, which I said I would take, even before knowing how much it was.

The altitude in that part of Guatemala is considerably higher compared to the jungle of the lowlands. The air was not heavy and humid as it had been the past several days. I walked slowly, so slowly in fact that mothers walking with their small children in tow passed me on the sidewalk. I had nowhere to go and I just wanted to take in the old colonial atmosphere of Antigua at a leisurely pace. I felt safe and didn't feel the need to constantly look over my shoulder or scan the street from side to side as I had for much of the trip to that point. Antigua was one of the more touristy areas of Guatemala and was generally safe, to my knowledge anyway. I wandered aimlessly, rather enjoying doing nothing.

I awoke the next day to the realization that it was the eighth anniversary of my proposing marriage to my wife. It made me think of how I missed her and the boys. I had proposed on the beach in Koh Phi Phi, Thailand, effectively on the other side of the world from where I now sat. It seemed like forever ago.

A day trip to Panajachel from Antigua, I discovered, was not a particularly good idea from a time perspective. The shuttle to pick me up was on "Guat" time, meaning it was late, oh so very late. Travel time was said to be one-and-a-half hours according to the guidebooks. This is very much *not* the case. The road to "Pana," as it was called, was like the one to Hana, Hawaii – too many switchbacks to count. It was up, down, up, down, up and eventually way, way down. Had it been a straight highway it would have taken twenty minutes but it ultimately took two hours more than that. The beautiful countryside rolled by, interrupted periodically by small towns that seemed to have entirely too many automotive shops, car washes, and mechanic services; for over two hours the only humanity I saw were those that offered things from pit row. It was truly odd to not see any restaurants or any other kind of shops. With gasoline at over $1 (U.S.) per litre I was surprised to see so much focus on the almighty automobile.

Eventually we crested a hill and as we came down I got my first glimpse of Lake Atitlán, the deepest lake in Central America. My eyes went to the horizon where the volcanoes in the distance provided a sort of wall, stopping the dark blue water below from running amok. The lake sits in a deep caldera, formed by a volcanic explosion thousands of years ago. Atitlán means "at the water" in Nahuatl, informally known as Aztec, and it most certainly is *at the water*.

The town of Panajachel itself is a jumble of compact streets littered with shops offering artisan goods for sale, one stall after another after another. I felt almost smothered as I walked the streets taking it all in. The streets should have been busy with visitors, as the town serves as the lake's main tourist zone, but alas they were few and far between. Vendors were fairly passive, infrequently yelling out to me as I walked by. In fact they seemed to be primarily selling to each other, perhaps more out of need at that time of year.

As I watched I noticed that many of the women had various goods stacked on their heads. It seemed the older they were – and there were a few that needed walkers or some form of motorized assistance – the larger the stack of textiles piled on their heads. Some had baskets but most carried the ubiquitous scarves, wraps, and blankets I was used to seeing. The other item that seemed to be everywhere was the cell phone. Regardless of age every female and most males had one, either stashed in a pocket or pressed up against an ear, eager to hear what was going on in someone else's life.

My first couple of attempts at renting a canoe were turned down with "You have to rent in San Pedro." This was followed by "I take you to San Pedro in private boat?" The private boat was much faster than the public boat and could take any gullible tourist to San Pedro, on the other side of the lake, and back for about as much as it would cost to stay at a discount hotel for a week. It seemed everyone wanted to give me a boat ride somewhere, even if it was only fifteen minutes away. I must have said "No, gracias," a hundred times. A simple canoe rental seemed rather difficult so I dropped the idea.

Later in the day as I sat people-watching at a hole-in-the-wall café I continued to think of Isabelle. I pictured what the trip would have been like had she been with me. It gave me a strange feeling in my stomach and my chest. I felt like something was missing.

So much of my life for so many years had been shared with her that it felt odd to be somewhere without her. I thought how certain aspects of the trip were actually easier because I was alone, particularly finding and selecting hotels – something she tended to spend a *lot* of time doing. The difference in our taste was minor; the difference in our level of comfort was massive. She would not have stayed at any of the places I had stayed on the trip to that point.

Even so, I missed being able to share with her both the awe and frustration I'd been feeling. I would normally have shared my daily ups and downs with her and I felt a kind of emptiness inside not having had the chance to do that. Certainly there were things I liked to do that she didn't and vice-versa but not having the chance to debate it or even discuss it left me feeling somewhat hollow.

As a general rule I hate to shop. It is one of my pet peeves. I am a hunter – I know what I want and I go get it. I don't search around for my prey at various stores and debate whether the $2 I could save if only I spent $3 on gas driving to the next mall would be worth it. I don't worry about the $2 or the $20. I enjoy casually shopping but only with Isabelle when there is no time pressure. Strolling around local shops and trying on locally made attire was something I actually enjoyed with her. I had spent exactly two minutes in shops since leaving Toronto and that was to buy t-shirts for Sam and Will. This type of activity connected Isabelle and I and I had missed that. I missed the inevitably ill-fitting clothes that made either of us look ridiculous and the resulting outbursts of laughter that would result. I missed the looks of surprise at the cost of things simply because we were foreigners. I missed watching her look around with a smile on her face as she simply enjoyed herself.

As I strolled through the streets I decided to go into a tiny bookshop. I picked up a copy of Paulo Coelho's *The Devil and Miss Prym*, a parable of a community struggling with the choice between good and evil. Somehow Coelho's book struck me as a dark and entertaining tale and I thusly coughed up the equivalent of a modest dinner in order to have something to read for a couple of days.

I must have been on Santander, the main street in town, just as school let out. The street was suddenly swarming with kids ranging in height from my knee to my waist. I had immediate pangs for my sons back home. I missed them more and more as the days passed. I wondered what they might be doing that day and a smile broke out on my face.

At the base of Santander is the lake. A large group of teenaged boys had clogged the street as I tried to navigate it. They were dressed for gym class – t-shirts, shorts, and running shoes. It turned out that the gym was actually the lake. Within minutes they had stripped down to their shorts and piled into the lake as if it was the start of a triathlon. Dozens of them splashed mightily as they did laps around a cordoned-off area. I got tired just watching them. As a terrible swimmer myself I looked on with admiration as they pulled themselves through the murky lake water stroke by stroke. My guidebook advised against actually swimming in the lake due to its being heavily polluted by endless boat traffic. The muddy Panajachel River drains into the lake also and I was not at all tempted to set foot in it either.

As I continued my walk around town I passed by a number of empty restaurants. They may have been full at another time of year but there were very few tourists to be found on that day. In front of one restaurant a couple of young men, sharply dressed in collared white shirts, approached and asked if I'd be interested in lunch.

"No, gracias," I replied.

"How about some ganga, then?" one of them said.

"No, gracias," I again replied.

"How about some chicks?" the other posed.

"No, gracias," I said for the third time. Business must have been really slow to offer that trifecta in the middle of the day.

I learned of the history of the area in the extremely small museum in the Don Rodrigo Hotel. It was an enjoyable twenty minutes perusing scale models of the lake and surrounding

A Most Improbable Adventure

volcanoes and discovering how it was the Spanish that forced the development of the towns that ringed the lake. Prior to their arrival the locals tended not to form settlements. The Spanish came and created towns with a church in the middle and then created a grid system of roads surrounding it. As I walked around I pondered the impact the Spanish had had on the ancestors of the people I passed in the street. It was difficult to conceive of the dramatic shift in lifestyle it must have been – from unsettled to settled, with a meaningless structure at the centre of their new world that these invaders seemed to care about greatly.

I awoke early the next day for a visit to the popular Pacaya Volcano. I was surprised to see that the shuttle van was completely full with people when it arrived. It didn't seem that the town was overflowing with tourists so I only expected a couple of others to be joining me. Included in the group were the two young couples that were on the bus ride from Flores to Guatemala City; they had taken a cab to Antigua while I had waited for the shuttle van. They were from Germany, it turned out. There were two other sets of Germans, a couple from Mexico and two guys from Japan. I've always been intrigued by the cultural make-up of tours. It always gets me thinking about the United Nations for some reason. There is something special about people from all points on the globe getting together to do the same thing, if only for a few hours.

The ride from Antigua to Pacaya was not nearly as nerve-wracking as the one to and from Panajachel but it was anything but straight and flat. The shuttle van was not built to seat people comfortably, let alone long-legged people like me. There was not a square inch of free space in the van so the temperature rose quickly, causing condensation on the windows, obscuring the view completely.

I sat next to one of the four young Germans traveling together. Her name was Valerie and she was distractingly attractive. Her eyes were a very light blue, her hair golden blonde, her lips full and her teeth nothing short of perfect. I found it easier to not look directly at her as I immediately lost my train of thought when I did.

"How long will you be in Antigua?" she inquired, casually curling her dangling hair behind her ear to reveal her bright, beautiful eyes.

"I plan to leave tomorrow for San Salvador," I replied.

"We're going to Lake Atitlán for a couple of days."

"Oh, I was there yesterday, in Panajachel. Where are you going after that?" That's when I looked directly into her eyes and paid absolutely no attention to her response.

"How long are you traveling for?" I inquired after regaining my composure.

"Well, we're all medical students and just finished a four-week internship in Belize. Now we have another four weeks to make our way to Panama City."

"I'm heading to Panama City myself. I started in Mexico City and have five weeks total."

"When do you leave Panama City?" she asked.

"October fourth. How about you?"

"We head back to Germany on October twelfth."

"How did you get an internship in Belize? I met another German while I was in Tikal who had spent two months on an internship in Guatemala City working for Starbucks. Is it common for students in Germany to do internships overseas?"

"Well, our medical school lasts six years and we have to do several internships over that time. They can be overseas or at home in Germany. We chose Belize because it was a place I had never heard of and they speak English there. We got the internship on our own just by making contact with a clinic there."

"That's amazing. So what types of things did you do in the clinic? What did you treat?"

"I treated everything from skin conditions to hypertension and diabetes."

A Most Improbable Adventure

"Wow," I replied, perhaps a bit too enthusiastically. "Was it a walk-in clinic?"

"Yes. The best part about it was that we had a lot more responsibility than we are normally given in Germany. There, all we do is watch. In Belize I got to do whatever I felt needed to be done. If I wasn't sure how to proceed I would just ask a doctor."

"What a great experience. Did you like Belize?"

"Yes. The people are so open and friendly. It's such a unique place."

"Do you mean all the cultures that co-exist there? Like the Mennonites and Maya and Garifuna?"

"Yes, it's so unique!"

"I thought the same thing; such a special mix of people."

I made direct eye contact again so I lost touch with the conversation for a minute, or two, or twenty, I'm not sure. Eventually I tuned back in.

"Your English is absolutely perfect, no accent at all," I said, hoping she had not just asked me a question.

"After high school I spent a year in the U.S. working as a nanny."

"Oh, that must have been interesting. Where did you live there?"

"Maryland. I did go to Canada once, to Montréal for New Year's for a couple of days."

"Montréal is where my wife is from."

"Oh, I really liked it there."

"It's a great place. I'm there often because I live in Toronto."

"What do you do?"

"I'm a travel writer and author. I'm sort of working right now."

"That's cool. What do you write about?"

"Well, I do freelance writing about the travel experience. My first book was about a trip around the world I took with my wife."

"Do you write guidebooks?"

"No," I chuckled. "I use them, I don't write them."

"So you're writing about your trip through Central America? Maybe I should get your contact information. Maybe we'll see something you write?"

"Sure, here's my card. I should get your information too, once we stop swinging and bouncing around in this van."

"Sure."

After getting her contact details I settled in—to the degree that one could actually get settled in such a van—and pondered the life of these young people as the ride proceeded up the volcano. They spent several months over the course of their six years in medical school doing short-term internships – all of which could be overseas if they wanted. My feeble mind struggled with how much of an impact that would have on them as they got older. Again I considered the things I passed up when I was that age rather than take advantage of potential life-changing opportunities. For a brief moment I felt anger building in me – anger toward myself. At the same time I was jealous, extremely jealous of them. These four intelligent, worldly young doctors-to-be, unknowingly and through no fault of their own, had managed to piss me off. Of course my rational mind knew it was not them that *made* me angry; it was me who made it happen. Clearly my anger was still brewing inside and it chose the jealousy of others as the trigger to rear its ugly head. Of course, I didn't let Valerie in on my little secret.

After finally reaching the head of the hiking trail we all poured out of the van. We were immediately met by a half-dozen rough looking men on horseback. I had heard that the trail was a prime spot for thieves preying on the steady stream of tourists going up the volcano so I assumed these men were some form of security that the fee I paid was going towards. They may well have provided some protection for us but they were clearly there because they wanted to be our four-legged taxis. There were no takers in the group but that didn't stop them from riding along beside us for the next fifteen minutes, asking if we wanted to forego the upcoming "difficult" climb and get a ride instead.

Larry, our guide, spoke only Spanish so I didn't catch much, nor did the Germans or Japanese. In fact he was speaking to only three people – the Mexicans and another German who also spoke Spanish. His role was to get us to the top in one piece, I supposed, and he was successful in doing so.

Pacaya had spewed lava off and on for several years prior and thus a huge swath of real estate was nothing but black rock with the occasional hot spot or vent that released steam into the air. Larry, who had gathered a handful of branches and sticks on the way to the top, went on to create a small fire from the heat of one vent and then toasted up some marshmallows for us.

As we all stood around pondering the moonscape I felt a tap on my shoulder. I turned to see Larry, motioning the other direction and suggesting I take a look. I couldn't believe my eyes. Another nearby volcano, El Fuego, a 12,000-foot monster, was erupting, blowing rocks, smoke, and ash into the air. Larry seemed almost disinterested in the scene once it caught my eye. Because he seemed extremely casual and calm about it I inferred that this type of thing was so common around here that it really was no big deal. With that in mind I was rather calm about it myself, catching the expulsions on my camera and a short video on my phone. I was impressed but because Larry was so nonchalant my awe was somewhat subdued. I figured if it was truly something amazing the local volcano guide would be impressed. Nonetheless, I stood and watched each belch as the ash billowed out, a dark, heavy grey colour that faded into light grey as it reached higher and higher into the sky. Because we were several kilometres away the whole scene seemed to unfold in slow motion. After only a few minutes the smoke had reached several kilometres into the deep blue sky.

That evening I was speaking with Isabelle via Skype and told her about what I had seen. She asked if anything happened in Antigua, which sits at the base of El Fuego. I said nothing had happened and it didn't seem to be a big deal around town. She told me about a big volcanic eruption in Guatemala that she had heard about on the news. She asked if it was the same one I had seen. I said I didn't think it was the same one, again because I heard nothing locally. In fact, it *was* the same eruption and it was international news for a few days as 33,000 people were evacuated. I didn't hear any rumblings about it in town after coming back from Pacaya because the lava came down on the opposite side of the volcano, away from Antigua, necessitating the evacuation of people in the villages below.

That night, after my Skype call with Isabelle, I made my way to a place called Sunshine Grill, a pizza joint with a Canadian flag painted on its façade. I entered and asked to see the owner. A man then appeared near the bar to greet me.

"My name is Edgar, how do you do?"

"Hola, my name is Jason; it's nice to meet you."

"How may I help you," he asked.

'Well, I'm from Canada and I noticed the Canadian flag outside so I thought I should come in and check it out."

"Oh, well, that's great," he said. "I lived in Canada for nearly twenty years before returning back to Guatemala to open this restaurant."

"What did you do in Canada?"

"I took the institutional food program at Humber College in Toronto. See there; that's my certificate of graduation form Humber," he said as he motioned to the tiny, framed certificate on the wall of the dimly lit place.

Edgar was a robust man of medium height, likely in his late forties and was very happy to discuss Canadiana with me.

"You see, I have a hockey stick here, a Labatt's Blue clock over there, and a Canadian flag over there," he said with a broad smile on his tanned face.

"You must get a lot of Canadians in here," I inquired.

"Oh, yes, plenty of Canadians stop by. They see the flag outside, just as you did."

"And how is business?"

"It's been great since I opened the place about seven years ago now. Tourists always want to know that the food is prepared hygienically and that the water is good and that the standards are high. When I tell them that I studied and worked in Canada they know that we do things right. They are more comfortable knowing this."

We chatted for a few more minutes about Canada, about my trip through Central America, and, of course, the great food at his restaurant. I wasn't in the mood for pizza so I took my leave, wishing him well.

In search of other Canadians in Central America I made my way to Café Sky, reputedly owned by a Canadian named Tom. In a rather brief and broken conversation with a waiter there I learned that Tom was not in that night but that I should ask for him at his other restaurant, La Canoa (the Canoe) on the other side of the tourist zone in Antigua. Sadly, Tom was not there either. It was simply not meant to be that particular night.

When I had previously bought my bus ticket to San Salvador I was told the shuttle would pick me up at 9:00am, the ride to Guatemala City would be about an hour, and the bus would leave for San Salvador about an hour after that. That seemed reasonable to me. The shuttle actually did show up right on time and the ride to Guatemala City was about an hour. The problem was that the bus for San Salvador left not one hour later, but four. The bus terminal was not much larger than a coffee shop but it did have Internet terminals so I took a chance and Skyped Isabelle.

Luckily we connected. Sam showed me dozens of pictures of animals in the book he was reading. Will stared at the screen for a moment before realizing he was looking at his daddy and then his face exploded with a massive two-toothed smile. He said "da-da" (or something I interpreted as such) and my heart nearly broke right there on the spot. He was so cute and happy I wanted to reach right through the screen and hold him tight. I missed having him in my arms and rocking him to sleep with his head on my shoulder.

"I've decided not to go to Honduras," I told Isabelle. "I'm just going to pass through on the way to Nicaragua."

"Why?" she asked.

"I've spoken to a few other travelers and each has said it's too dangerous right now."

"Really? Why?"

"I've heard that there is too much violence and people are being robbed and attacked, especially tourists. I'm sure it's not as bad as all that but I've heard it now from several people and I just don't want to take a chance. It's not worth it."

"Well, it's probably better to play it safe and just skip it. It's not worth risking it."

"The U.S. State Department has apparently called Honduras the most dangerous place on earth. I spoke to a few Australians the other day and they told me that they heard stories of people being attacked with knives as they stepped off the buses at the terminal. That's a little too much for me. I'm just going straight to Nicaragua after El Salvador." What I did not mention to her was a tidbit of information I had discovered about Honduras: it had the highest murder rate in the world – over 90 per 100,000 people – double that of the next worst country on this ominous list, Venezuela. Canada, in contrast, had a murder rate of 1.5 per 100,000; the U.S. rate was 4.7.

"I just want you to be safe, Sweetie."

"I will be. I'm stuck here in this little terminal for a few hours though."

"Just make the best of it and go with the flow."

"I will. Can you get Sam again so I can say goodbye?"

"Hi daddy!" he said with his usual 3-year-old enthusiasm. I'm playing with my cars right now."

"That's great, Super Sam. I just wanted to say goodbye. I'm going on a bus to another city soon so I have to say goodbye for now."

"Okay, daddy. I'll talk to you soon, okay?"

"Okay, buddy. I love you."

"I love you too, daddy. Bye." Again my heart felt heavy.

The screen scanned across the kitchen at Isabelle's parents' house. She appeared again, this time with Will in her lap.

"Travel safe, Sweetie, and let me know when you arrive, okay?"

"I will, Sweetie. Big hugs and kisses to all. I miss you."

"I miss you too. Talk to you soon."

"Bye. Love you."

"Love you too. Bye."

After I logged off the computer I turned and made eye contact with a lady I had seen earlier as we stood in line to get our bus tickets. I noticed she had a Canadian passport. I walked across the terminal and sat down beside her.

"Hi, my name is Jason. I noticed earlier that you had a Canadian passport. I'm from Canada too. Where are you heading?" I inquired.

"Tapachula, Mexico," she replied.

"What's happening in Tapachula?" I inquired.

"I need to leave the country for a few days before I can come back in. I've been on tourist visas for the past six months but I need to leave in order to get a new one when I come back in."

"I see. The visa run."

"Yes, that's it exactly."

"So where in Canada are you from?"

"I'm actually from London, England, but I lived in Canada for nearly twenty years."

"Really? I just met a guy in Antigua that lived in Canada for twenty years also before coming back to Guatemala."

"I loved living in Canada – it's a great country. I'm travel living now; I have been for the past four years all over the world."

"What is travel living?"

"Well, I've lived on a boat, I've camped, and I've moved from place to place whenever the mood strikes me, whenever the energy needed to be freed."

"The energy needed to be freed?"

"Yes, I'm an energy healer."

We spoke for the next hour about energy, meditation, travel, life in England, Canada and elsewhere and through it all I never got her name.

I must have had my stupid switch set to "ON" when I ordered some chicken and rice from the lone kiosk offering food at the terminal. I was hungry and it looked good. I ate it rather quickly and didn't really think too much about it. I then passed the time reading my travel guide and my Paulo Coehlo book, and before long it was time to go. Of course, there was no announcement made. People just got up and started moving outside to a waiting bus. I noticed "San Salvador" tags on some luggage near the cargo hold of the bus so I figured I was in the right place.

Part way through the trip I started feeling nauseous; nothing terrible, just enough to feel uncomfortable. I reached into my bag and took out the package of Gravol I had brought with me. I popped one into my mouth and followed it with a few peanuts I had left over from the last bus trip. My nausea was not getting better and after a few minutes I started to feel cold, and then hot, and then cold again. The saliva started to pool under my tongue. *Oh shit, I thought, I'm going to have to throw up right here in this smelly bus.* I stood up from my seat and carefully made my way to the back of the bus. I pulled as hard as I could on the bathroom door, to the point that when it finally gave way I nearly fell over backwards and lost my cookies right there onto an unsuspecting passenger. That's a hard one to explain, in any language.

A blast of extremely hot and densely humid air hit my face. The rancid, overpowering smell of toilet cleaner immediately shot up my nose and triggered the inevitable. For the next five minutes I heaved into the bowl—a hole really—launching every last possible solid and fluid I had in my stomach. The bus rattled incessantly and careened around corners, throwing me from side to side as I tried to stay centred above the hole. I grabbed the sink for dear life and was able to stabilize for long enough to finish the job and gain a bit of composure before stumbling back to my seat. I settled in for a few hours of bumpy, rattling, tossing and turning before we hit the border crossing into El Salvador.

When we stopped the bus was boarded by a female border agent. She was pleasant enough and spent less than two seconds looking at me and then my passport before handing it back. She seemed to give the others a harder time, engaging in some rather lengthy and animated conversations. After she left the bus a couple of well-built men in army fatigues made their way through the bus, firing looks of suspicion at nearly everyone. They interrogated several people, checked a few pieces of luggage, and then went on their way. Was this a sign of things to come in El Salvador?

MEMORY AND TRUTH

Before long we arrived in San Salvador and I could not get off that bus fast enough. As my feet hit the ground I felt all momentum and movement stop. My head was still swimming but my stomach had settled and it felt wonderful to be standing still on solid ground. Everyone else got their bags and departed quickly, like bugs scattering from under a rock that had just been lifted. Everyone, that is, except me, who clearly was the only foreigner and the only one who had thrown up along the way. I quickly realized I was standing there completely alone, in the dark. The bus had departed and I must have looked rather dazed. Out of nowhere a young lady appeared and approached me.

"Taxi?" she inquired.

"Si," I replied. "Hotel Villa Serena Escalón, por favor."

She quickly pulled out her cell phone and, in the most rapid Spanish I had ever heard, spoke to what must have been some kind of dispatcher. She turned to me and said I don't know what but I did understand "Seis dólares." Fine, I thought. I wanted out of the dark and into a comfortable bed. I simply nodded and smiled. A few minutes later a taxi arrived and I was back in motion.

The hotel seemed nice enough, once past the iron-barred gate. I checked in with relative ease. After I settled into my room I went to the common area of the hotel where I saw

Nancy, the school vice principal from Chicago whom I had met earlier in my trip in Caye Caulker, Belize. She and I had kept in touch as travelers tend to do when they are taking much the same route through foreign lands. She smiled and said, "You made it! Have you eaten?"

"No," I replied. I had a rough ride."

"Well I saved some leftovers for you. I bought some avocados, rice and pupusas."

"What's a pupusa?"

"It's made of a thick corn tortilla, cooked pork – ground up into a sort of paste – and refried beans."

"Great, I'll give it a try but my stomach is not in great shape."

I got a plate from the small kitchen and started to eat. I felt a little better right away. My stomach settled and the light-headedness began to fade.

"How was Antigua?" Nancy inquired.

"I liked it. It was a quaint town. I think I would have enjoyed it more if Isabelle was there. She would have liked it too."

"So, you saw the Fuego eruption up close? I saw your Facebook post with the picture. That must have been cool."

"Yeah, it was cool. I didn't realize it was such a big deal until later."

"Yeah, it's been all over the news."

"At the time I thought for some reason this type of thing happened a lot so this was no big deal but I was told later it was the biggest since 1999."

"Wow, that's pretty special. Nothing happened when I was there but I really liked Antigua too."

"Where are you off to now?"

"I leave for Managua at five in the morning."

"Five! That's brutal. That won't be much fun."

"I know. I'm not looking forward to it. I want to go to León though so I may do a day trip or something."

"I heard León was the place to go. I want to head there myself but I'm going to hang out here for a few days first."

"Well, I'd love to chat some more but I have to get up at three in the morning so I'd better go to bed."

"Okay. Let's stay in touch."

"Will do. Goodnight."

"Goodnight."

With that I was again on my own, eating avocados and rice, and hoping it stayed down, before I crashed into bed for some much needed rest.

I had no real plan the next day other than to venture on foot toward the historic district and see a few landmarks. I still wasn't feeling great so I didn't want to overdo it. I headed out in sweaty-hot and humid heat at ten in the morning and started walking one of the main thoroughfares. I had a map with me just in case I found myself lost in what is often referred to as a very dangerous city. I found myself walking extremely fast. It was broad daylight but I still felt the need to move quickly.

After walking a few blocks I could hear noise in the distance. It sounded like the drums and horns of a marching band. As I turned a corner I saw thousands of people lining the street, many waving the flag of El Salvador. I had stumbled onto an Independence Day parade of rather massive proportions.

Marching bands banged out the tunes while young girls twirled batons and others danced and jumped in their costumes. Families with small children crowded the sidewalks looking for a good place to watch the passing parade. Every third person, it seemed, was selling something: water, gum, fruit, pupusas, coconut milk in a bag, just about everything. After fighting my way through the sweaty madness I found a way to cross the street.

Leaving the parade behind I came across a new mass of jumbled humanity: street vendors in a congested market. The smell of urine, vomit, vehicle exhaust, and trash began to envelop me. My stomach started to turn. I wasn't able to focus much on my stomach however as I was so focused on not bumping into anyone or anything as I tried to navigate the ever-narrowing street. As I stepped over piles of trash and streams of sludge I had to dodge cars and trucks and vendors pushing carts of fruit. Young children, some in diapers and barely able to walk, seemed to be everywhere, clinging to the pant leg of a parent. I was bumped several times by passers-by and vendors selling everything from toilet paper to cell phones. I felt like a pinball on a slanted table with no way out.

As I made my way through it all the near deafening sound of air force jets and then helicopters required that I look up, which caused me to almost trip over yet another pile of trash. Just as I regained my balance I almost stepped on a homeless man splayed out on the sidewalk. If he wasn't dead he was close to it. His arms and legs lay in a twisted tangle, his face laying cheek-down on the dirty sidewalk. He was deeply tanned and wore nothing but a pair of tattered shorts. His ragged and natty beard obscured his face so I could not see if he was breathing. His chest was not moving as it should for someone alive, or clinging to life. People walking down the sidewalk from the opposite direction stepped over and around him as though he was a piece of freshly chewed and discarded gum. I had only a brief moment to adjust my stride to avoid stepping on him without causing the many people behind me to run me over. After I passed I glanced back, hoping that the image might somehow have changed but it hadn't. I thought I should go back and make sure he was okay. Then I considered what I would say and realized there was nothing I likely could say, in any language.

As I approached the Catedral Metropolitana (Metropolitan Cathedral of the Holy Savior) an extremely old and tiny woman jutted her hand out toward me, cupped in the hopes of receiving some loose change. Just then a young woman zoomed past balancing a tray full of cakes on her head. *Cake? Really? It's a thousand degrees out here. Who wants cake?* Around the corner, toward the entrance to the church, sat a woman breastfeeding her baby. Beside her stood another child, barefoot and wearing nothing but a soiled diaper. I ducked into the church ahead of another fruit peddler who was heading my way. Although the thought of a piece of cool watermelon was a compelling one I thought better of it.

Expecting the solace and quiet I was used to inside the sanctity of a place of worship I was quickly disappointed. The walls of the church must have been made of paper because the noise inside was exactly that of the noise outside. I heard a mumbled prayer being spoken in the chapel to my left but the din of honking horns, screaming vendors, sputtering buses, and the occasional aircraft drowned it out handily. In the pews of the main nave sat only a handful of faithful, many of which, it seemed to me, were just looking for a place to sit down away from the chaos outside. I sat in quiet contemplation for a moment before being interrupted by a man hobbling around on a crutch. His right leg had been amputated below the knee and the rags that masqueraded as his clothes seemed ready to slide off his impossibly frail body. He mumbled something incomprehensible to me and then hobbled away.

I generally find churches to be quiet spaces with slow moving energy. They enable me to slow down my breathing, my heart rate, my thinking. This particular church offered none of what I had become used to and none of what I sought that day. An elderly man in the pew in front of me had slumped forward, nearly falling out of the pew completely. His head, with only a handful of wispy, white hair, bobbled to and fro as he breathed in and out, gently snoring as he exhaled. Clearly he had found what he was looking for.

Just as I started to settle in the tiny old woman who had thrust her hand toward me outside the church appeared at my side. She mumbled something and stood, rather *struggled to stand*, awaiting some sort of response. I looked up at her and gently said, "Lo siento, no." Her eyes were a lifeless brown and did not change whatsoever based on what I had said. She simply moved on to the couple that sat in the next pew over. She was waived away by the man before she had a chance to utter a sound.

The noise, the begging, and the dead energy eventually got to me. Despite the significant effort on my part to get there, I left. Pope John Paul II, twice, and U.S. President Barrack Obama had previously visited the Cathedral – I wondered what their opinions may have been. Maybe I was being too harsh.

I spent the next several minutes trying to find a way into the Teatro Nacional, which was supposed to be rather spectacular on the inside, but to no avail. A boy of no more than eighteen years of age stood behind the barred entrance wearing a security uniform and carrying a sawed-off shotgun in his hands. It seemed the theater was closed. I then asked myself what the point was of coming to San Salvador. It seemed to have limited things to offer and from what I had seen to that point there was no reason to stay.

On my way back to my hotel I made my way to Parque Cuscatlán in which stood Monumento a la Memoria y la Verdad (Monument to Memory and Truth). Almost 300 feet long, the monument lists, on a black granite wall, the names of nearly 25,000 Salvadoran victims of civil unrest in the 1970s and 1980s. Although locals breezed past it like it was a bus stop I stood quietly for some time in front of it trying to comprehend it all. It was, in my mind, the Vietnam War Memorial of El Salvador and it was sobering to see those thousands of names carved so perfectly in the stone. As a young couple kissed rather passionately on a bench nearby I walked, slowly for the first time all day, by each panel, noting the year and feeling the shock of the number of names under the heading Homicidios. It seemed an awful lot of life to be lost that way. It struck me odd that the monument slowed me down in a way that the city's most important historical sites could not. Nothing seemed to be more important than those names, at least for those few fleeting moments.

Before long it was time to fight my way back to my hotel, clear across town. The streets were by now filled with military trucks and troops. Thousands of people were making their way down the street, away from the parade route, and opposing my attempts to make progress. The military presence, I guessed, was likely two-fold: participate in the celebrations of the day and also make sure nobody did anything stupid.

As I made my way up the street toward my hotel I noticed a group of people crowded on the sidewalk. Clearly they were watching something interesting. Being inquisitive I decided to check it out. I was surprised to see an elderly woman—she was eighty-five if she was a day—dressed in a schoolgirl uniform, sporting a tight-fitting top and extremely short skirt. *That's odd, I thought.* What she was doing, however, was even odder: dancing to *Macarena*, the truly annoying hit song from the 1990s. As she gyrated and made all the requisite moves the song demanded I fully expected her to snap a hip and end up face down on the pavement. Amazingly, she put on a stellar performance that would have made a woman half, quarter, or eighth her age very proud indeed. The crowd clapped along and gave her a rousing ovation when the song ended. She smiled broadly; sweat pouring down her face, muddying her plentiful makeup. The crowd then began to disperse.

I continued on my trek. Eventually, sweating and out of breath, I spotted the Scotiabank sign, an indication that my hotel was close. I rounded the corner and nearly sprinted the few metres to get to the barred gate that was the hotel entrance. With a loud buzz and snap the gate unlocked and I darted in. That was enough for me for the day. I wanted to rest in San Salvador, to gain my strength, and get my stomach back, before going on to Nicaragua. I hopped in the shower to wash off the filth and grime that had attached itself to my sticky-hot skin before settling in at the hotel's lone functioning computer to do a little research on the coming days of my Central American adventure.

Rafael, the front desk clerk, had said I should come to him at seven in the morning to talk about buying a bus ticket to Léon, Nicaragua. I knew Tica Bus, the main bus carrier in Central America, had a bus going to Managua at five in the morning, the one Nancy had taken the day before, but I had no desire to go to Managua. All I had heard from other travelers was that Managua can be skipped, and Léon was the place to go. It was on the way to Managua but I wasn't sure if it was possible to go directly there.

Rafael, a kindly young man that spoke serviceable English, greeted me as I approached the front desk with a broad smile. His slightly pudgy but pleasant face was nice to see after another sub-par sleep.

"I already called Tica Bus this morning, sir," he said with a certain amount of pride.

"And what did you find out?"

"There is one at five in the morning to Managua in economy class but also one at three-thirty in executive class."

Disappointed in the lack of new information I tried to not let my being pissed off come through in my tone. "Yes, Rafael, I knew that. Is it possible to get directly to Léon or do I have to go all the way to Managua?"

"Let me call again, sir."

"Okay, great. Gracias." I stood nearby while he made the call. He got through and began jotting down the same information we both already knew.

"It is only Managua it seems, sir. You can go to the, how do you say, terminal, and pay there."

"It's not possible to pay over the phone?"

"No, you must go there."

"Can I pay at San Benito Terminal?"

"Yes, sir."

"Okay. Can you call me a taxi please?"

A Most Improbable Adventure

"Okay, sir."

I went back to my room to get my wallet and passport, muttering to myself how it shouldn't be that difficult to get a bus ticket. A minute later the room's phone rang; my taxi was there already.

I hopped into the taxi and said, "Cuánto a Tica Bus San Benito?"

"Seis dólares," he replied. He went on to say something else that I interpreted to mean he would wait for me and bring me back.

"Doce dólares," I confirmed.

"Si," he replied.

"Okay." I was anxious to have the ticket in-hand so I could mentally get ready to go to a city I didn't really want to go to at a time of day that was simply awful.

I knew something wasn't right the second I saw the Tica Bus office completely closed up, tin sheets that looked like garage doors drawn over the entire place. *Fuck, I thought. We're either too early or the place is closed today.* It was Sunday.

"Terminal de San Carlos?" I asked the driver.

He had an exasperated look on his face. I didn't want to go back to the hotel and waste more time. "San Carlos?" I repeated.

"San Carlos," he said as he turned the key to fire up the engine. Away we went across town to the other Tica Bus office. We arrived at about twenty to eight in the morning. It was closed, too. The driver got out and spoke to a security guard at the building next door and came back to the window of the car.

"Está abierto a las ocho," he said, again looking exasperated. "Veinte minutos."

"Si, veinte minutos," I acknowledged, disappointed.

He hopped into the front seat, started the car, and proceeded to park it more safely on the sidewalk. We waited. Amazingly, a young Tica Bus employee showed up at around ten minutes after eight. I quickly bought my ticket not bothering to ask about León because the man spoke no English and I couldn't piece together the right words in Spanish. I was going to Managua the next day.

I was grateful to the driver for taking me to two places and waiting an additional thirty minutes. I offered him $15 and he seemed pleased. I was sure it was enough to cover the entire day for him under normal circumstances.

I jumped out of the taxi with a heartfelt "Muchas gracias!"

"De nada," was his quick reply.

In the end I paid $15 in order to buy a $30 bus ticket; one that would take me 500 kilometres, cross two international borders, and take at least twelve hours.

Later that day I made my way to Galerias de Escalón, the modern shopping mall not far from my hotel. When I tire of a city I often go a place that provides a bit of modern comfort and this mall did exactly that. It could not have been a more opposite experience from the previous day. After stumbling over trash and through sludge the day before I found myself 24-hours later in the lap of luxury. The mall had every brand-name store and convenience conceivable, spread out over four levels of shopping heaven. I actually hate shopping, but I like air conditioning and I like Starbucks (don't judge me).

In all my travels I had not seen a Starbucks of such magnitude. It was at least twice as big as a typical Starbucks store and had a large patio that overlooked the second level of the mall, providing an expansive view all around. It was there that I saw the only other tourists I saw in all of San Salvador – two older Japanese men were hungrily downing the huge frappuccinos they had in hand.

It occurred to me that the obvious economic disparity that existed in San Salvador was no different than anywhere else I had ever been: India, Egypt, South Africa, Colombia, Cambodia, Brazil, and many others. I had seen everything from the ultra-rich and obnoxious to the destitute and downright devastated. In any city or country there are the haves and have-nots. This knowledge somehow made me feel less anxious about sitting in Starbucks in what was surely the nicest mall in the entire country while I still had images in my mind from the day before. There were no barefoot children, no elderly beggars, and no destitute homeless people in the mall. Rather than dwell on it, and feel even worse, I told myself to just accept it and move on.

The rain fell for hours as I flip-flopped in bed that night. The lightning cracked right beside my head and the flash came a few seconds later. The open-vent windows to the outside ensured a restless sleep and also proved to waste the enormous energy expended by the air conditioner, which itself whipped up a noise like a helicopter at close quarters.

There's nothing like getting up at quarter after three in the morning in order to catch a bus for a twelve-hour ride. It just didn't seem normal, or even humane for that matter. Some things are torturous and some are stupid. I wasn't sure if this didn't perhaps qualify as both, especially given what had happened the last time I was on a long-distance bus ride only a few days before.

Bleary-eyed but always punctual I was at the front door at 3:45am when my taxi was supposed to have been there. Alas, I was forced to wake Rafael from what looked like a restless sleep, his head resting across his forearm across the desk.

"Carlos ordered me a taxi for three forty-five but I don't see one," I said, jarring him awake.

"I'll check again, sir," he replied sheepishly, barely awake.

I took this to mean that he would call one, rather than check to see about the one that should have been ordered.

"Five minutes, sir," he said, with a reassuring smile.

"Okay, I'll just go get the rest of my things from my room and I'll be right back."

I wasn't in my room for more than a minute when the phone rang. Rafael informed me, with what I can only describe as glee in his voice, that the taxi had, indeed, arrived.

"Tica Bus San Carlos," I said to the driver before he had a chance to ask.

"Siete dólares," he replied.

I couldn't have cared less if it was seven or ten or more, I just wanted to get to the terminal and get out of Dodge. Fortunately, there was little traffic at that ungodly hour in San Salvador and it took mere minutes to get to the terminal. I was surprised to see two other passengers there ahead of me. After sitting for only a few minutes a man instructed us, I assumed, to get on the bus, and so we did. The three of us sat in the 52-seat bus by ourselves when it pulled away, long before the 5:00am departure time. My feeble mind struggled to process something happening *ahead* of schedule in Central America.

As the bus rumbled along through the dark streets of San Salvador my stomach continued the dance it had begun back in Guatemala City, days before. I decided to pop a Gravol and hope for the best. A few minutes later we pulled up in front of the Tica Bus terminal in San Benito – the very same terminal I was dropped at when I had arrived in the city and that which was closed when I went to buy my ticket. The bus was quickly filled with what appeared to be a cycling team from Nicaragua, perhaps *the* cycling team. Several of them wore t-shirts indicating some sort of competition was held that weekend. Most of them were boys, really, with the exception of the coaches. They settled in all around me, including right beside me, and immediately they all pulled out their cell phones and began making those all-important five-in-the-morning calls. They all looked like they were ready to go out to a bar: fashionable clothes, earrings, hair slicked up and back (for speed?), and the occasional baseball cap – tilted sideways of course.

As we rumbled out of town my stomach thankfully settled down. I actually slept for about an hour before being awoken by the chatty-Cathy sitting beside me as he leaned over the seat in front of him to playfully discuss matters of great importance with his friends.

A Most Improbable Adventure

The temperature in the cabin of the bus dropped to 17°C and the windows were so fogged up it was impossible to see outside. Fortunately, I had been warned that particular bus would be extremely cold so I was prepared with long pants and a long-sleeved shirt. Before long we had arrived at the Nicaraguan border. For some reason, however, we spent over an hour sitting in the bus waiting to get *out* of El Salvador. The driver dashed in and out of the bus a few times but otherwise there was no movement at all. We simply sat in our seats waiting for something to happen. It always struck me odd how difficult it often was to get *out* of a country. Shouldn't you just be able to walk/drive/fly out fairly swiftly?

After finally being allowed to leave El Salvador we drove ahead for a few seconds and parked in order to enter Honduras. The bus driver came back into the cabin and asked each person for their passport or other form of identification. Many years ago I had a hard and fast rule about never letting my passport leave my sight. I often got into fights over my stance, delaying many entrances and a few exits as well. I gave up that rule during my trip around the world several years before as I realized I would get nowhere unless I relinquished it at border crossings. It was common practice in many nations to take passports out of sight of their owners and I had gotten used to it. As the driver reached for my passport I recalled my former stance for only a moment and then I handed it over. *What could he do with it that would cause any problems anyway?*

After he gathered all the documents the driver disappeared. Within a few minutes he got back into his seat and we were off. Passing through Honduras at its southernmost point took only a couple of hours. The entire time I was *sans passport* but, then again, so was everyone else on the bus; somehow that made me feel better about the whole thing. Before long we had arrived at the Nicaraguan border.

Prior to this adventure my knowledge of Nicaragua consisted largely of the much publicized Iran-Contra affair that dominated the airwaves in the mid-1980s. Some bungling American authorities decided it was wise to sell arms to Iran (the same country whose enraged citizens had occupied their embassy in Tehran only a few years earlier) and used the proceeds to fund the Contras – the anti-Sandanista rebels in Nicaragua. It was not a pretty picture.

The Americans, of course, had occupied Nicaragua since 1912 and had backed the much hated Somoza regime for decades before the Sandanistas put an end to it in 1979. This revolutionary war took thousands and lives and left the country in despair. The Sandanistas instituted numerous programs and policies—of the left-leaning flavour—that brought literacy, education and healthcare to the forefront. The Americans, naturally, were not big fans of the Sandanistas and therefore the CIA began supporting the Contras, many of whom were former members of the Somoza's National Guard, themselves originally trained and armed by the U.S. military. The Sandanistas were eventually ousted from power via elections in 1990, though they remained on the scene as an opposition party. Later they again came back into power, led by the enigmatic Daniel Ortega.

What kind of country was I about to enter? What lingering effects would remain after the revolutionary and civil wars? Would there be any signs that it happened at all? I was intrigued to find out how the decades of tumultuous and halting development had impacted Central America's poorest country.

THE DANE AND THE KIWI

The bus pulled up to a run-down old building that was surrounded by vendors of all sorts, all of whom pounced when we exited. We were told, I gathered, to get our bags from the hold under the bus and go in to the rickety old building in front of us for inspection. After finally getting my backpack, and fighting my way through the dozens of men offering me "great rates" on currency conversion, I got in line to show whoever may be interested that I was not trying to smuggle anything awful like maple syrup or back bacon into their country.

After we waited almost an hour standing in the sweltering heat a border patrol agent finally appeared. He was a frail old man who struggled mightily to walk. He shuffled toward the inspection table unbearably slowly; the collective groan from all in line was audible. We all knew it was going to be a long afternoon. I glanced around in anticipation of seeing a much younger version of the old man, hoping against hope that said individual would increase the team's average speed dramatically. Sadly, the old timer worked solo.

As I watched him work my spirits lifted. He had everyone unzip their bags while still in line and then he took a cursory glance inside each after they were heaved onto the table. He looked as closely as a bouncer would look at the driver's license of a young girl going in the back door of a dance club. The most he did was shuffle around a few garments and look underneath a package. He glanced inside my smaller backpack as I held it open for him and then barely looked in my larger one before flicking his bony wrist to waive me on. *Now that was tight security.* After being questioned like a criminal, and felt-up (in a bad way) entering many countries, especially the United States, Nicaraguan security seemed like a joke.

After all was said and done nearly thirteen hours had passed by the time we rolled into the terminal in Managua. My assessment of the city, informed only by the passing houses, shops, piles of trash and wild dogs via the window of the bus, confirmed for me that there was no reason to stay there and I should head straight to Léon. I just didn't have enough of an interest to stay in a city described in my travel guide as follows: "Managua is a strange place. It has an eerie ghost-downtown surrounded by anonymous neighborhoods pockmarked with volcanic craters and criss-crossed with streets that lack character as well as names." It goes on to say: "The city is a frustrating, bewildering place and easily the least accessible, hardest-to-negotiate, and toughest-to-discover capital in Central America." And to top it off: "If the city seems like one big accident, that's because it is." Not exactly a glowing recommendation.

Rather than use a single ounce of energy to try to find reasonable accommodation nearby the terminal or elsewhere I decided on the spot to stay at the Tica Bus Hotel conveniently attached to the terminal. It took less than a minute to locate the front desk and get a room. I opted for the so-called executive room, which included a private bath, air conditioning and a television. I said yes before I even knew how much it was. It didn't matter at that stage.

Indeed, there was nothing *executive* about the room at all. It was a tiny, plain, room with two single beds and a 13-inch T.V. with colour and contrast issues. Surprisingly, however, the shower did have hot water, and it didn't smell of sewer or garbage. The towel, however, smelled of raunchy sweat, which I actually preferred to the smell of gasoline that was so prevalent

A Most Improbable Adventure

in other hostels and hotels. It was also of medium abrasiveness rather than the high-grade sandpaper I was used to that often left my more delicate parts of bit raw afterward.

I struggled to get to sleep. I thought about what I had done to that point in the trip, the things I had seen and the people I had met. I thought about my future plans, where I would go next, and how much time I had left. I tossed and turned, read a book, watched T.V., tossed and turned some more and eventually fell asleep on the three-feathered pillow and concrete slab that was the softer of the two single beds.

Thanks to Edgardo, the very helpful young man at the front desk, I knew I needed to get a taxi to UCA (he pronounced it "oooka"), the University of Central America, where I would catch a mini-bus to Léon. I was told I could catch a taxi to UCA right out front of the terminal which itself was tucked away in a mostly residential neighbourhood on a beaten-down road surrounded by nothing but other dilapidated buildings. I was so used to being attacked by taxi drivers everywhere I went it felt truly odd to step out of the terminal and not be approached. I actually had to stand and wait for several minutes as the lone taxi driver finished his engrossing conversation with someone and noticed me.

"UCA," I replied to what I assumed was his question.
"Ah, UCA. Vas a Granada?" he asked.
"No, Léon," I replied.
"Léon, si."

As he swerved in and out of relentless traffic and up and over mammoth speed bumps he informed me, "Granada es mas linda que Léon." (Granada is more beautiful than Léon.)

Well, thanks for telling me that. Why would you say that? I had heard Granada was beautiful but that Léon was very nice also. I hated the idea of going somewhere I wasn't going to like – I had already done that already. I suddenly felt very defensive about my decision. It was one man's opinion of course, why did it matter? I was planning to go to Granada afterward anyway so why was the opinion of one Managua taxi driver so important? Ultimately it wasn't important of course but I couldn't quite put my finger on why his comment affected me so much.

Within minutes we had arrived at UCA and the chaos that is the jumble of chicken buses, shuttles, vans, taxis and even horses that amassed there, picking up and dropping off thousands of people in a convoluted and frantic mess. Thankfully he knew where exactly to go as I was nearly stunned wondering where to get out if he had asked me. He pulled up to a new-looking 15-passenger van and hustled me out of the car with baggage in hand. I felt like a dignitary rushing from a limo to a waiting helicopter, dipping my head to make sure the spinning blades didn't take my head off. I paid him, spun on my heel, and saw a rather angry-looking and decidedly ugly old man at what looked like a ticket kiosk.

He shot a cursory glance my way and turned back to shuffling a few papers. I'm certain I saw a sneer on his face, as though I had done something to really piss him off already. I took that as my sign to not approach him and turned to get in through the open door of the van. The noise of the street quieted ever so slightly though I could hear the voice of a man who I assumed was the driver petitioning passers-by with a repeated staccato: "Léon, Léon, Léon!" Slowly, people started filtering into the van, mostly women.

Before long the van was full and we backed out and jetted off. I assumed I would pay at some point. I knew it was only $2 or so and considered that this rate may get inflated the further we went before I actually paid but I had not seen any of the locals pay yet either. Even if the rate had doubled I could not have cared less; it was cheap. Where else in the world can you pay $2 to go a hundred kilometres in relative air-conditioned comfort anyways?

After about an hour, and a harrowing ride where we passed all manner of transport in various stages of serious disrepair, we stopped at some sort of home-made kiosk. There, two heavy-set women jumped up from their chairs and approached the van offering an assortment of dumplings, tortillas, fruit and other goodies. It was at that point the other passengers started rooting around in their purses and wallets. The driver started collecting the fare, snapping the cash out of extended hands. I timidly offered my $2 wondering if there may be subsequent demands. I was almost surprised when no further request came.

As with all unscheduled, unregulated, untaxed, and unpredictable transportation schemes the driver later pulled over several times at the behest of passengers looking to be let out at non-descript corners here and there. I was confused as to whether to get out or not, as the van, once full, was now nearly empty. I motioned to the driver as to inquire if I should get out too. He looked at me rather confused and flicked his hand as he turned away.

"Hostel Lazy Bones," I said, hoping to get his attention, and more importantly, an acknowledgement that we understood each other. He didn't flinch. I hoped he got my point. I supposed I would find out eventually. The streets became increasingly more crowded, noisy, and run-down. I thought for a moment that he'd drive right past Léon and onto some other town and then suddenly he jerked the wheel to the left and darted down a compact side-street. The fact that he was mere inches from running over a rickety old cart, drawn by perhaps the skinniest and most feeble looking horse I had ever seen, did not faze him. A few equally alarming turns later and we had arrived at a scene similar to that in Managua: chicken buses, vans, and taxis scurried about like kernels of corn popping in a hot pot. I had arrived, it seemed, in Léon; a city reputedly not nearly as beautiful as Granada.

I hadn't put both feet on the ground yet before taxi drivers boldly entered my vaunted personal space, offering cheap rides. Once I pushed my way through the mayhem to get my backpack—which can conveniently be used in lieu of elbows for clearing space—I turned to the first taxi driver next to me and said what must be the most sought-after word in their business: "Si." I then shoved my way through the rest—this was no time to be too Canadian. Gentle, polite and courteous have no place in these types of situations.

"Cuánto a Hostel Lazy Bones?" I yelled to be heard over the ruckus.

"Dos dólares," he yelled back.

"Dos dólares?" I repeated.

"Si."

His uninviting taxi was cramped, dirty, and smelled of a toxic brew of sewage and urine that sent my nose hairs a flutter but I got in anyway. My options weren't going to get better and I had to acknowledge that a raunchy odour has never stopped a taxi from going from point A to point B. I was looking forward to arriving at my rather randomly selected hostel so I could get out of the insanity for a moment. The driver stopped several times along the way as people flagged him down, eventually taking a middle-aged man into the front seat who obviously going the same direction I was. I chuckled at the notion of the first-world taxi with a light atop the taxi indicating its availability. Availability in most other places in the world was indicated simply by its presence on the road. Moments later he jerked the car to the right, jammed on the breaks to bring us to a very rapid stop, and pointed his left thumb out the window, mumbling something that included the word "pronto." I took that as my sign to get the hell out, now.

The hostel had a steel gate for a door, not particularly attractive, and, after standing there for a few minutes it finally popped open, with the buzz of a security door releasing. Inside the space opened up and I could start to picture what it must have been years before – a horse stable.

"Hola," came a very pleasant female voice. I turned and was disappointed to learn that the face did not match the voice.

"Hola. Tiene una habitación para esta noche?"

"Sí."

"Tiene baño privado?"

"Sí."

"I'll take one of those."

She motioned for me to wait as she ran down the long length of the entrance and courtyard. I took this to mean she was getting someone who spoke English. A moment later a young woman appeared but seemed rather annoyed. She briskly asked me for my beloved passport and showed me the room. It was, indeed, a horse stall, or at least it used to be. The roof sloped sharply and the simple bed and night table sat there rather wishing there was something else in the room to keep them company, it seemed to me.

"Esta bien," I said. "I'll take it."

The rest of my day was spent wandering the streets of Léon, taking in the sights and sounds of the bustling streets. I made a brief stop at the Centro de Arte Fundación Ortiz-Guardian, a museum that displayed pieces from the fifteenth century all the way to Picasso and the present day. I was, naturally, completely alone in the place. My twenty Córdoba donation apparently kept the doors open for the entire day. I later discovered the appealing Casa Café, ordering my usual drink and relaxing for a few minutes as I explored.

The very old and slightly worse-for-wear Catedral de la Asuncion, which is the centrepiece of the city, drew my attention to its upper reaches where stood several men, chiselled from rock, with their arms positioned above their heads appearing to hold up the church itself. A stroll inside was less than spectacular, though the nave was rather grand in length. The cathedral is billed as the largest in all of Central America. Clearly it also attracted wild dogs, as they scavenged the area looking for scraps and napping lazily outside the entrance. One of them, I feared, was dead; it was in such desperate shape. There was no movement, no breathing, and it had a cold stare in its unblinking eyes. After a few moments it finally showed signs of life and eventually moved to a new spot before settling back down on the ground and falling asleep.

After wandering a few streets over I stood with map in hand and heard a voice from above. Well, a voice from above and behind, anyway. As I turned and looked up I saw the figure of a young white man in a doorway behind a set of bars.

"Do you need any help?" he asked.

"No, thanks, I'm just getting oriented."

"My name is Colin. If you need anything just come by."

"Where are you from?"

'Pennsylvania. How about you?"

"Canada. Toronto."

"Ah, not that far."

"What is this place?"

"It's a foundation and also a Spanish school, amongst other things. I'm the general manager."

"Wow, what brought you here?"

"Well, my wife is from Nicaragua, for starters."

"Interesting. Maybe I'll pop by tomorrow."

"Anytime."

I made my way to the bank, hoping to exchange the Guatemalan Quetzales I still had in my pocket. I stretched my limited Spanish the best I could, trying desperately to get my point across to the young woman teller. I was hoping to exchange them into either Dollars or Córdobas. Alas, I was not able to do either. "No es posible," I was told. I had the opportunity to change it when I entered El Salvador but I wanted to wait until I would surely get a better rate, but the better rate never came.

I stopped by a tour operator's office to inquire about volcano boarding – apparently a popular activity with travelers looking for a unique, and perhaps just a little bit dangerous, experience. Volcano boarding is pretty much what it sounds like – riding a snow board on black, volcanic sand down the side of a volcano. Having never actually snow-boarded either I thought riding down the side of a volcano would be pretty fun. I went into the office and found a very happy looking young man with a broad smile on his face.

"Hola. I'm interested in going volcano boarding. How many people do you need to have enough for a tour?" I inquired.

"All we need is one more person and we can go tomorrow morning," he replied.

"So, I'm the only one in the whole town that wants to go?"

"Let me check around at some of the hotels and see if there is someone else who wants to go," he said.

He then dialed the phone a couple of times, firing off incredibly rapid Spanish – so fast that I didn't understand a single word beyond "Hola."

"It doesn't seem there will be enough people tomorrow," he said, rather dejectedly. "Let me get your information anyway, just in case," he offered.

I told him where I was staying and he jotted it down on the starkly blank sign-up sheet.

"If you want, you can come by before we close tonight and see if someone else has signed up. We close at six-thirty tonight."

"That's a good idea. I'll drop by before you close."

I returned to the office at 6:15 just to be safe. Upon arrival I was greeted by a very securely closed door and iron bars. I took that as a clue that nobody else had signed up and I was not going to be gliding down the side of a volcano tomorrow. I knew it was low season for tourists, I just hadn't realised it was *that* low.

I then headed out to find something to eat. The streets were quiet as the sun went down. Very few people were about and even fewer restaurants appeared open. I stumbled across a hole-in-the-wall that seemed to be open so I went inside. All I found was a griddle and a propane tank. I was very much alone. I stayed anyway, as I didn't feel like walking around for hours trying to find something better. The angry woman who sat me also cooked the rather greasy quesadillas and then proceeded to watch me eat; perhaps concerned I might dine and dash for a couple of bucks. To add true authenticity to the moment a tiny, brown Chihuahua scampered across the floor periodically, chasing ghosts it seemed. I could not eat fast enough. I shoveled the quesadillas into my mouth, chewed twice, and swallowed. After inhaling the plate in its entirety I dropped an enormous tip, relatively speaking, on the table and bolted for the door.

I awoke slowly the next day after a groggy and restless sleep. I shuffled along the stable floor and stepped into the shower. Cold water slowly drizzled out of the shower head. The Hot knob was broken, it turned out, and the Cold knob was largely ineffectual, only somewhat increasing the flow of cold water. After about two minutes I wasn't feeling groggy anymore.

I made my way to Desayuno, a breakfast place on the corner. I was greeted by a smiling older gentleman but served by a very angry young girl. I'm not sure but I think she told me to screw off when I placed my order for yogurt and granola. I spotted my first tourists, other than the three people I saw at the hostel, in the restaurant and they didn't look very happy either. With my dreams of boarding down the side of a volcano dashed I resigned myself to simply strolling around town and visiting its many churches and parks. It was early in the morning but already extremely hot and humid.

Inside Iglesia de San Felipe I sat in the very last pew quietly taking in the atmosphere of the sacred, old (built in 1685) and very empty space. I encountered no one inside the church – at least initially. As I sat, relaxed, with my eyes closed quietly repeating a meditative mantra to myself, I heard a shuffling and grumbling sound. My first thought—admittedly not a rational one—was that one or more of the statues of Jesus in one of the six glass cases in the church decided to come to life. My heart skipped a beat and I may have let out a barely audible, and brief, eight-year-old girl scream. When I regained my senses I realized it wasn't one of the Jesuses; it was a homeless man who had set up his bed in one of the pews in front of me.

A Most Improbable Adventure

After a quick moment of shuffling he settled and fell silent. I tried to get back into my meditative state but I couldn't stop thinking about those statues of Jesus in various states of anguish. Suddenly I didn't feel like hanging out there anymore.

As I continued my exploration I stumbled into a lively market where various vendors scurried about and screamed at passers-by. Stalls and carts were laden with everything from fruit to clothes to used toys. Nothing had a posted price; it was the local economy functioning at its very best. As was the case over the past several weeks I was the only traveler to be seen. Because of this I expected to be the target of many aggressive vendors. I was, however, left completely alone. It was as if I wasn't even there. I felt oddly invisible.

Back at Casa Café I sat in quiet contemplation – staring at my café mocha and feeling the breeze of the spinning fan above my head. I thought about Earl, my brother Colin's best friend, who had passed away a few months prior. I immediately thought of my brother, and my heart sank. He was in pain, I knew it. I grabbed my phone and sent a text:

> *Brother, I hope all is well with u. I'm sitting in a coffee shop in Léon, Nicaragua and wondering how u are doing. I've been thinking of Earl… don't know why…I think I miss him…and I miss u too.*

His response:

> *I'm still working through the Earl thing. I think about him every day, still in denial I think. Wish I was there with you.*

My eyes started to tear up. My lips quivered as I held back what was sure to be a sob had I let it out. My chest ached. My heart was broken thinking about my brother and his devastating loss. I would have paid anything to be sitting across the table from him right there in Léon, of all places. I sat for several minutes, letting the emotion pass, calming down. I realized then that this entire adventure allowed me the space to grieve Earl's passing. I silently wished Colin the capacity to grieve also. I felt his pain deeply and knew he was still in shock from it all. He held onto the pain likely not wanting to let it go for fear of losing his connection with his best friend. I closed my eyes and sent him the energy I knew he needed to work through it. I don't know if it helped but I felt connected to him in the process and the ache in my chest began to subside.

Whether it was because he shared the same name as my brother I'm not sure but I decided right then to stop by and see Colin, the young man I had met the day before while walking around town. When I arrived he was in a meeting so I sat and waited.

"How can I help you?" he asked, emerging from a back room a few moments later.

"Well, I'm a travel writer and, amongst other things, I'm writing an article about expats in Central America. It's about Canadian expats but I thought you might have an interesting story to tell."

"Can you give me a few minutes? I just need to wrap something up," he said. "In fact, maybe we could talk over lunch, I'm starving."

"Absolutely. I'll wait right here."

A few minutes later he appeared and we were off. Joining us was his wife, Yuri, who also worked there. We walked around the corner and down the block to a restaurant that had its menu outside not in the form of the written word but in the form of a large cart laden with buckets full of rice, beans, and all manner of meat. Colin ordered for me—he had learned Spanish, I discovered, while in Nicaragua—and we all sat down for lunch.

A Most Improbable Adventure

As I sat sweating profusely from every conceivable pore in the sweltering mid-day heat, despite being in a covered courtyard, they seemed rather comfortable. I was intrigued to hear their story so I jumped right in.

"So, how did you two meet?" It was an ice-breaker type of question for most conversations and to most it's meaningless and boring and nobody listens to the answer anyway. I, on the other hand, *was* interested. It intrigued me to no end to find out how an east coast American kid met, fell in love with, and married a Nicaraguan girl.

"Well," Colin started, "when I graduated University in tourism I was looking for an internship and found one at a hotel on Small Corn Island here in Nicaragua."

"Of all the places in the world," I jumped in, shaking my head in wonder.

"I know. I couldn't have imagined such a place. Luckily I got a position there. Yuri was a dive instructor there. One day we were walking home from the hotel, simply to walk home, not because there was anything going on between us, and suddenly we were kissing beneath a tree."

I've always loved stories that have the word "suddenly" in them. It usually denotes the fact that all sorts of stuff happened before that moment, but somehow the storyteller felt it was the kind of stuff that was either uninteresting or stuff that would somehow expose them. *Suddenly* was a great way to skip ahead in the story and get to something titillating, like kissing under a tree. It was all very *sudden*.

"Oh, suddenly you were kissing," I joked.

Both of them laughed a guttural laugh and made eyes at each other across the table. Colin was slightly-built, medium-height, light-haired and blue-eyed while Yuri was heavier-set with dark skin and full lips. One thing I had learned over the years was that sometimes seemingly odd pairings are anything but.

"So, when was that," I inquired.

"I came out to the Corn Islands in January of 2008. I had a girlfriend at the time but I went back to the States and broke it off with her."

When he said this I could see in his eyes that he was the type of guy to do the right thing. In that moment he had won me over as an honest man who clearly loved his wife.

"We didn't get together right away," he added. "We were friends. We got married in April of last year and we are expecting our first baby next year. We're ten weeks along already."

I was nearly taken aback at how much he was sharing with me. It gave me a strange sense of belonging. Perhaps he always shared openly with strangers but I felt a little special. Given they were only ten weeks along I felt even more a part of the club since the general rule is to tell people only after reaching twelve weeks.

"Wow, that's fantastic! Congratulations!"

"Thank you, thank you," he said, again making eyes at Yuri across the table.

"Thanks," Yuri quietly added.

"So how did you end up here in León?"

"Well, we were both looking for a new opportunity, outside of tourism. I had met the director of the foundation years before and stayed in touch with him. I told him I was looking for something new. He was able to bring me on to manage the tourism aspect of the foundation and now I'm the general manager as well," he said with pride in his voice.

"That's a big change from working in a hotel," I said, pointing out the obvious.

"Oh, yes, it's quite something. The foundation is amazing. It's focused on finding the root cause of the kidney disease so many workers in the sugar cane industry suffer from. In addition, we have a Spanish school, do homestays, and manage many volunteers who work on various projects. There is a lot going on. I have a lot of responsibility that I wouldn't have had in the tourism industry."

"And how did you learn Spanish," I inquired.

"We both learned just by immersion," he replied.

"Now, wait," I stumbled. "Yuri, did you not learn Spanish growing up?"

"No," she replied. We spoke Creole, you know, English." Only recently they implemented Spanish as mandatory in the schools. The government realized that nobody in the Corn Islands could speak Spanish. My parents barely understand it and my grandparents not at all. I learned some along the way and the rest by immersion."

"So, it's a bit like Belize, then," I reasoned.

"Somewhat, yes," she replied. "I lived in Belize for a year. I have a number of family members living there."

"Now that's an interesting country, isn't it?" I said.

"Have you been?" she asked, with a hint of surprise in her voice.

"Yes, I spent a few days there on my trip."

"Where did you go?" she inquired.

"I spent a few days in Orange Walk and Caye Caulker."

"Orange Walk, where's that?" Colin jumped in.

"Well, I didn't know where it was either until I got there. And the reason I even went is because of a girl I met on a bus ride from Mexico City to Chetumal. She was from Orange Walk and told me to go, so I went. Her uncle owns a hotel and I stayed there."

"Wow, that's why you went?" Yuri said.

"Yes, and that's how I met my first Canadian expat," I replied.

"What? How did that come about?" Colin asked.

I went on to explain how I met Doug, the restaurant owner and entrepreneur who made a business of bringing up 200-year-old trees off the bottom of rivers in Belize and Panama. They reacted as I did at the time – in disbelief. I went on to tell them about my improbable meeting with the Canadian filmmaker who directed and produced the first ever full-length film made in Belize with an all-Belizean cast. Their eyebrows rose even further.

"I know it sounds incredible, but those are just two of the people I have met so far on the trip I'll be writing about. I'd like to include you, too. I think your story is fascinating."

"Well, that's very cool," Colin added.

"Tell me, when your baby arrives will you stay here in Léon, or will you move closer to family? I know the challenge of having kids and not being close to a family support network. My wife and I live in between my family and hers and it can be difficult."

"We don't know yet," they both said, almost simultaneously.

"We don't usually plan more than a few months ahead," Colin confessed. "We could do any number of things. Raising a child is going to be a challenge regardless of where we are. We'll figure it out."

I was impressed with how down-to-earth and centred they both seemed. He was twenty-six; she was only twenty-three. I couldn't imagine being where they were at that age, with that type of responsibility about to be thrust upon them. When I was twenty-six I was focussed on much different things – like Friday and Saturday nights.

"I'm forty-one and I have two young boys, one is three-and-a-half and the other is eight months old. I know it can be a challenge – like nothing you've ever experienced. People will give you all sorts of insights and advice but there is absolutely nothing that can prepare you for what you are about to experience."

"I know," Yuri said with trepidation in her voice, and her eyes.

"I don't mean to scare you. It will be amazing, and, along with that, things you've just never experienced."

I had, as I spoke, a longing in my heart for my sons. My mind flooded with flashbacks of Sam as he grew; it happened so incredibly fast. Will was growing too. I had been away only a few weeks but to a small baby that was a huge amount of time.

"You don't look forty-one," Colin jumped in. "You seem in such good shape and don't look forty-one." My ego got a nice stroke.

"Yeah, you don't seem that old at all," Yuri added.

"Well, thanks. I had kids much later than you're going to. Your circumstances are much different than mine. Tell me; is the health care system good here, for having a baby?" I realized the second I said it that I had judged what I could only assume to be an inferior system relative to what I, and Colin, would be used to. I wished I could have taken back my rather rude question. It was too late.

"It's not bad," Colin jumped in, allowing me to save face.

"It's not great though," Yuri added. "I mean, it's not clean. Hospitals should be clean but they aren't."

"The system has worked for me," Colin added. "I broke my ankle last year and it was okay. The hospital was dirty, yeah, but everything turned out fine."

"I'm sure everything will be great. They've been having babies here for a long time so I'm sure everything will be just fine," I said, attempting to back myself out of the corner I felt I had put myself in. I really was sure they were going to be just fine, too. They had a great energy about them and I was amazed at what they were doing. They were scraping by on extremely limited incomes and they were about to have a baby; plus they were basically kids themselves. I was in awe. They seemed to be handling it all with grace.

We stayed and continued chatting about babies, jobs, parents and parenthood, the foundation, families, my first book *Around My World*, and various other topics, as any long-lost friends would. It was a thoroughly enjoyable two hours and not something I was likely to forget any time soon. Despite their arguments against it I paid for lunch, a large expense for them though it was only a few dollars. We promised to stay in touch as we shook hands and said our goodbyes.

The trip from Léon to Granada was to be two short shuttles with a change in Managua. Why there wasn't a direct shuttle was never adequately explained to me, in any language. Nonetheless, it was to be in two parts. I sat nearly comfortably in the middle of the first row of seats in the shuttle van to Managua. The driver, much like his colleague who brought me to Léon in the first place, was not averse to the idea of passing other vehicles he could not actually see around while negotiating blind corners, going uphill. Of course, there was nary a gasp from the passengers as all this transpired because they were all likely used to it. But, alas, I was not. Being the only foreigner I was the only one who seemed concerned for everyone's safety. The driver seemed indifferent to the whole exercise, especially as he casually slipped his seatbelt *off* once we left city limits. Oh yes, that seatbelt must have been a major distraction.

I didn't think I would be but I was happy to see Managua when we arrived. The jumble of buses and vans clustered together stood just across the street from the very peaceful and tranquil looking campus of the University of Central America (UCA). I hadn't even stepped out of the van and screaming offers of Taxi! Taxi! Taxi! were thrown at me in rapid succession from all directions. After fighting my way out of the van I quickly grabbed my backpack from under the seat in the back and turned to one of the yelling taxi drivers and said "Granada?" He jerked his thumb a couple of times, indicating that I should go left. So I did. I hadn't taken ten steps when an elderly gentleman materialized and yelled at me, "Granada!" I responded with a nod and he swiftly—with agility and deftness that defied his advanced age—pulled my backpack from my hand and flung it into a nearby bus that hadn't yet fully stopped. He shouted in my face one more time, "Granada!" and then shoved me through the open door of the bus as it continued to move forward. He wasn't polite but he was effective.

I quickly scanned the bus in hopes of finding an actual seat, not wanting to have to sit in the aisle. The curious eyes of about forty people checked me out from head to toe and back again. I had a brief moment of panic as I replayed in my mind what had just happened, trying to convince myself that I had indeed gotten on the correct bus – it all happened so fast. Unless the old man was just messing with me, yelling "Granada!" in my face, I should be okay, I reasoned. I dropped my gaze to an empty seat near the front of the bus. That's when I noticed the only other tourist, a blonde woman with a backpack so large it had a seat of its own. I quickly grabbed the empty seat a few rows behind her and plopped down, stretching my right leg well into the aisle.

We hadn't gone more than a couple of hundred metres before the bus pulled over to let more passengers on. I then realized it was not like the shuttles that basically go direct when full, this bus was going to stop all along the way. I had a brief moment of dread as I imagined the hundreds of stops we were going to make, thus making a very short trip extremely long. Slowly but surely the bus filled up with passengers.

At the next seemingly random stop a young woman got on with her baby. There were no other seats available so she readied herself to stand, holding the pole nearby with one hand and holding her baby in the other. I quickly moved over to the window seat so she could sit down.

"Gracias," she said with a broad smile.

"De nada," I replied.

She shifted her baby so that they faced each other, the baby on her lap. I glanced over to see the round and fleshy face of a young baby girl of perhaps nine months. She wore jeans and a pink top with a hood, beneath which I could see little earrings in her tiny ears. My heart melted. A smile broke out on my face as I stared – probably for a minute or more. She faced her mom, grabbing her sunglasses, making faces, and snuggling. Again I smiled and just took it all in. By that time I didn't care that I was staring – she was just such a beautiful child. Moments later, as I looked out the window as the landscape rolled by, I felt a tiny, warm caress on my right shoulder. By the time I turned the baby had removed her hand but my eyes met hers and I sensed that she was trying to connect with me. Maybe somehow she knew I had a baby at home about her age and she wanted to let me know that everything was going to be just fine. I locked on her tiny brown eyes for what seemed like several minutes and then she slowly rested her head on her mom's shoulder and gently closed her eyes, falling fast asleep. I immediately saw Will's face as he often fell asleep on my shoulder the exact same way.

A few stops later the woman got off. I was disappointed. In a fraction of a second someone took her seat beside me. It was an obese and sweaty woman that crammed me into a tiny space not meant for anyone over five feet tall. My knees were jammed into the seat in front of me and my hips were locked into the backrest of my seat – I was stuck. Within minutes of bouncing down the road my knees started to ache and hips began to burn as though I had been running a marathon. I shifted ever so slightly, trying to release the death grip the seat had on me but I was completely stuck; there was not a single inch to spare. I had to do something, but what?

The pain was increasing, and spreading fast – into my quadriceps and lower back. I was unable to move and feared my whole body might just seize up right there in that can of sardines and an emergency crew would have to be called to cut me out, possibly having to sacrifice a body part or two such that I might live on. After a while I couldn't take it anymore and did the only thing I thought I could do – I stood up. At least I tried to stand up. My legs were rammed into the seat in front of me so I partially stood up. I straightened my legs, picked my ass up off the seat, and rested the weight of my upper body on my right forearm as I rested it on the seat-back of the woman beside me. The immense pressure on my knees

A Most Improbable Adventure

and back began to release and blood started flowing again. I was still very uncomfortable but at least I didn't feel like I was going to die right then and there.

After trundling along for what seemed like forever—given my awkward stance—we arrived in Granada. The locals quickly evacuated the bus, leaving only the blonde woman and myself to figure out what the heck to do next. I overheard the driver say to her, "Parque Central" as he pointed ahead. I recalled from a map I had seen that the central park, or central square, was only a few blocks from where I assumed we were. The woman and I started to head in that direction. She put on her enormous backpack and walked with power and balance that rather amazed me. The pack must have been at least sixty pounds and she was not very tall so the pack made her look even smaller. I followed behind, heading toward the central square. I had in mind two potential hostels at which to stay, both of which were close to the square; I just needed to get oriented. Just as the square came into view she turned her head over her right shoulder and asked, "Where are you from?"

"Canada," I replied. "How about you?"

"Denmark. Where are you headed?"

"I'm not sure. I have two places in mind."

"I'm going to Oasis. I think it's just a couple of blocks from here."

"Oasis was my first choice. Let me get my map out to see where we are." I fumbled in my pack for a moment and took out my guidebook. I was pretty sure we were going the right direction.

"I think we need to turn here," she said.

"What's your name?" I inquired.

"Christina," she replied. "What's yours?"

"Jason. It's nice to meet you."

"You too."

We continued walking, attempting to step around street vendors, traffic, and trash. We quickly shared our stories—she had quit her job and was over four months into a year of traveling—while also focusing on finding the hostel before we both passed out from the heat and humidity. After a small detour—I believe the error was mine—we arrived at Oasis. Neither of us had reservations but there were plenty of rooms as it was very much low season in Granada too. I took a relatively expensive room; she took the kind of room that someone takes when they are traveling for a year.

Christina and I agreed to have lunch and check out Granada a little bit. She had been staying in Léon for the past ten days after nearly two months in Antigua learning Spanish and traveling around. She was 34 and was very happy to have left her job and life back in Denmark for a while. She had also spent two months in Mexico so her Spanish was quite good. I looked at her with a certain admiration as she ordered her lunch with ease, engaging in an actual conversation. Her English, of course, was perfect so I assumed she would eventually be perfectly proficient in Spanish too. I didn't know it at the time but Christina would become my travel companion, and interpreter, for my time in Nicaragua.

"A friend of mine is here in Granada doing a Spanish homestay. I'm meeting him tonight for a drink. Would you be interested in joining us?"

"Sure, that sounds great," I replied.

We met Phil in the square. He stood out even more than me, despite it being dark outside, because he was six foot four and towered over everyone. After introductions we made our way down Calle La Calzada and eventually parked ourselves on the outdoor patio of O'Shea's, the local Irish pub.

"Every town has one," I joked.

Phil was from New Zealand and was in his early forties with slightly greying and receding hair. His bright eyes and smile seemed to fit perfectly with his unhurried speech.

"How long have you been traveling?" I inquired.

"About a year and a half," he replied.

"Wow, that's a long time. Where are you off to next?"

"Well, I'm going to Costa Rica next, then Panama, then South America."

"How much longer will you be traveling?"

"About six months, we'll see."

He was so casual about it all I was almost put off. He spoke quietly, mostly with his eyes looking at the table. Maybe he was just shy. He and Christina went on to talk about common friends and where they were in the world. I watched them talking and sharing stories as we all munched on the largest plate of nachos I had ever seen. They were absolutely awful but I ate them anyway.

The topic of his going to Panama came up at some point. He was going to visit an old friend from New Zealand who had some sort of business in Panama City and was apparently doing quite well. Christina joked that maybe his business had something to do with the drug trade. We all chuckled. I imagined Phil's friend picking him up at the airport in an expensive car and whisking him away to an expansive guesthouse on a palatial estate where he would live a rich and famous lifestyle for as long as he wanted.

"No, I don't think it will be like that. My friend is a pretty regular guy," he said. "Although that reminds me of a time when I was traveling in Thailand. I had run out of money so I rang up my sister to see if she could wire me some. I spoke to my brother-in-law, who had business connections in Thailand. Anyway, he said he'd call some people. The next thing I knew a stretch limo arrived to pick me up. The driver jumped out and asked if I was Phil. I told him I was and he said he was there to take me to my hotel."

"What?" I blurted out. "Are you kidding me? A limo just shows up and takes you to a hotel. And you still have no money?"

"Right, I have no money and I'm standing there in a t-shirt, ripped shorts and sandals."

"This sounds crazy," Christina added. We both shook our heads briefly and then Phil continued.

"The driver took me to this amazing hotel and put me in a suite that overlooked Bangkok. It was incredible. He said that my brother-in-law was a long-time business associate of the family and that I would be taken care of."

"This is like a movie," I jumped in.

"Wait, it gets better," he said.

"Better?"

"So I end up meeting the patriarch of the family and the whole family greets me for dinner in this amazing house. In Asia they believe very strongly in family and in business relationships. My brother-in-law meant a lot to this 85-year-old man for that reason. So I was treated as a member of the family."

"Seriously, there can't be more, can there?" I questioned.

He smiled a little and said "Well, yeah, there's a bit more. One day they sent over a member of the family, a nephew of the old man, and he was to be my *social coordinator* while I was there. He was a fun guy. He loved everything American, just loved the culture. He wore a cowboy hat, jeans, and one of those huge belt buckles as big as a dinner plate."

"Get out of here," Christina jumped in. "Really?"

"Yeah, he loved the American lifestyle. His job was to take care of my social needs so he set up evenings out at restaurants, bars, everything. That was his entire job – he took care of people. He took me to all the best bars in Bangkok; I was living the dream."

"But you still had no money," I asked.

"Correct."

"So you're living in this amazing suite, you have a social planner and you have no money?" I confirmed.

"Right. And I forgot to mention something else. I also had a car and driver at my beck and call. They gave me a driver who would literally go wherever I wanted and would wait for me no matter where I was. It was this beautiful blue Mercedes."

"This is definitely a movie," I said, "or at least a book. You have to write a book about your travels," I suggested.

Phil smiled sheepishly and dropped his gaze to the table. His shoulders slumped inward just slightly and he brought his hands together in his lap.

"Well, I don't know about that," he said, nearly whispering.

"If you've got stories like this, and you've been traveling a lot, which I assume you have, you should write something," I encouraged.

"What about the rest of the story?" Christina jumped in, eagerly awaiting more.

"Well, one day, the social organizer guy, the nephew, showed up and said that they were moving me to a nicer hotel. He said the family was very sorry for the accommodations and that I'd be more comfortable somewhere else. So he took me to an even more amazing place – I think it was the Hilton or something – and I had a suite just below the penthouse. There was a pool in my floor! I had a corner suite with amazing views. I actually felt uncomfortable. I told the nephew that it was not necessary; it was too much. The nephew said it would not look good to turn down the offer so I almost had to accept it."

"Did you talk to your sister or brother-in-law during any of this?" I burst out.

"Yeah, I told my sister what was going on, more or less."

I interpreted that to mean no, not really. A smile broke out over Phil's face, confirming my initial belief.

"At one point my brother-in-law found out what was going on from the old man and not long after that he sent me an e-mail strongly suggesting I continue on with my travels."

"Your brother-in-law put an end to the dream?"

"Well, he thought it was best if I moved on, so I did."

"It was over? Your time as a member of the elite rich and famous of Bangkok was over?" I joked.

"Yeah, but that was alright."

I sat back in my chair, not realizing I had made my way to the edge of it as Phil's story progressed, nearly in disbelief. It really did seem like a movie.

"Yeah, it was a lot of fun," he said still smiling as he reminisced.

"How old were you when all this happened?" Christina asked.

"I was about twenty-five or twenty-six. Yeah, lots of fun."

All three of us sat in silence for a moment, mellowing in the afterglow. I hardly knew what to say. What could I possibly say that would be interesting? Phil broke the silence.

"What happened before all that was interesting too, yeah, I forgot to mention that part."

"What are you talking about? What happened before?" I asked, wondering if there was another amazing story in there somewhere.

"Well, I was staying on the beach in the south of Thailand, me and my friend, and we were hanging out with a couple of girls from England. One day we all rented scooters to go for a ride. The girls told us they had done it before but it turned out they hadn't. One of the girls had a really bad accident; really, really, bad. She lost control of the scooter and hit a sign post on the side of the road. Her leg, her shin actually, hit the pole and snapped the pole literally in half."

"Ouch," I said, as I cringed.

"Well, it snapped the pole and shattered the bone in her shin. There were bones and flesh hanging about, it was bloody awful. Yeah, it was awful. We quickly went to pick her up but her leg was in really bad shape. An ambulance eventually showed up, which of course was just a rusted-out old pick-up that was open in the back. We had to take the bikes back so we put her in the truck and met up with her later at the hospital."

He used air quotes when he said the word hospital, implying that it really wasn't much of one, which I expected.

"What happened at the hospital? Were they able to fix her leg?" Christina inquired.

"Well, all they did was give her some basic pain medication, like aspirin or something, and put a splint on her leg. They didn't really do much to help the situation. Her leg was shattered and she needed an operation."

"So what happened?" I nearly yelled, finding myself pulled into the story once again.

"Well, I rang up her travel insurance company to see if they would pay to get her to a proper hospital. We were in the southern islands and needed, really, to go to Bangkok for proper attention."

"Did the insurance company help out?" I asked, anticipating the answer would be no.

"No! They said they would send a specialist out to see the injury and verify it before they would pay for anything. I told them I was standing right there with her and that her leg was completely smashed so there was no need to send anyone out. They said they needed one of their approved physicians to see it in person, and that would take two to three days."

"Two or three days!" Christina said with surprise and disgust in her voice. I was thinking the exact same thing.

"Yeah, it would take that long to get someone down there. I told them that if it took two or three days then she would lose the leg. It would be infected in no time and need to be amputated. I argued with them but they wouldn't budge. That's the problem with these travel insurance policies – they're completely useless."

"So what did you do?" I asked.

"We talked about it some more and then I rung up the insurance company again to plead our case but they shot me down. In the meantime her knee had swollen up so big she couldn't see her leg below it. It was actually a good thing that she couldn't see it because it was bloody fucking awful. When she asked me how it looked I had to lie. 'Oh, it's fine,' I said.

'It will need a few stiches and you'll be alright. No problem.' I had to lie. It was awful."

"So how did you help this girl?" Christina asked.

"Well, I rung up my sister, to talk to my brother-in-law, because I knew he had contacts in Asia and I asked if there was somebody he could call. He said 'don't worry about it, just sit tight.' So I sat there with her, her friend, and my friend. In the meantime my brother-in-law had rustled up a private plane that could take her up to Bangkok. The girls had no money so my friend and I used up what we had, maybe four or five thousand dollars, to pay for the plane."

"Holy shit! Are you serious?" I blurted out. *This is a movie. This guy's life is a movie.*

"Yeah, she got to the hospital alright and the rest of us met her there several days later because it took us that long to get there. It was amazing really. This all happened so fast. It was about six hours from the time of the accident to the time she got on the plane. I was on the phone nearly constantly, coordinating everything. Yeah, it was quite amazing really."

"I hope this girl thanked you and paid you back," Christina chimed in.

"Yeah, the family came over to see her and they eventually paid me back. But that's how I ended up in Bangkok with no money."

"So that's when you called you sister to wire you some money and that's when you ended up in the limo and in the hotel suite with a social planner and driver. That's how it all began?" I gushed all in one breath.

"Yeah, that's how it all started. Well, actually, no, it started before that. You see, this girl, the one who shattered her leg, she was a bit accident prone."

"You mean the story goes even further back? This is like listening to the story of Star Wars; it's all happening in reverse," I said.

Phil smiled, chuckled lightly, shifted in his seat, and continued. "Well, yeah, we met these girls a few days before,

A Most Improbable Adventure

you see. My friend and I were walking down the road and we saw these girls near a swampy, marshy type of area. They were looking into this swamp like they saw something in it. There was a barbed-wire fence there so they were standing back, looking in. We came up and asked what they were looking at. They said there was a kitten in there. This girl really liked kittens so she wanted to go in and get it out. I told them not to try it because of the fence and because of the swamp, not to mention a bunch of trash and broken wooden planks that were in there. She was intent on it though and climbed through the fence to get this bloody kitten out.

"She had just stepped into this swampy mess when she stopped and said 'I think I've done something bad.' That's when I saw she had stepped on one of the wooden planks. It had a huge nail sticking out of it and she had stepped directly on it."

"No!" I screamed. "Ouch!"

"Yeah," he continued, "she had stepped right on it and it went clean through her foot and was sticking out the top. It wasn't very big in diameter but it was really long and it was stuck right through her bloody foot. My friend and I climbed in to get this plank unstuck and get her out of there. My friend held onto her and I heaved this bloody plank off, pulling the nail right back through her foot. It was bleeding like mad."

"This girl definitely was accident prone," Christina said, shaking her head.

'What about the stupid cat," I inquired.

"Funny you should ask that," Phil continued. "After I pulled the plank off I reached for the cat and then gave it to her to hold for a second before we left to go get her foot fixed up. Yeah, it was quite something."

"Did you go to the hospital then," I asked.

"Well, first we got it cleaned up with the supplies we had. She had her shots and everything. It just bled more. Fuck, did it bleed. We went to a clinic and they didn't do anything really, nothing more than we had already done."

"So *that* was how it all started. That was Episode I, the beginning," I mocked. "A girl steps on a nail, then you guys all start hanging out together. Later she shatters her leg. Was it the same leg as the nail?"

Phil sat for a moment, trying to recall this detail from fifteen years prior. "You know, I'm not sure," he replied. I laughed, not really expecting that he'd remember.

"So," I continued, "she shatters her leg. You pay to get her to Bangkok to a real hospital, thanks to your brother-in-law pulling some magical strings. You are then broke and call your sister to wire you a few bucks. Suddenly you are whisked away into the lifestyles of the rich and famous with a driver, palatial suite, and social coordinator. Does that sound about right? Does that about sum up the trilogy?"

"Yeah, that's about it. Yeah. It was quite something."

"Yes it was quite something," I repeated. "Thanks for that amazing story, Phil. You are quite the storyteller. You really should write a book."

"Well, I've been writing a bit over the past year or so. Yeah. I don't know what I'll do with it though."

"How much do you have?" I inquired with interest.

"Round about two hundred thousand words."

"Really? That's more than a book, that's two!" I replied, almost in shock.

"Oh yeah? I don't know. It's just my thoughts and experiences. I don't know who would be interested in reading that."

"It's for exactly that reason that people will read it. You definitely should do it. You're a great storyteller. I would buy whatever book you wrote."

We went on to discuss my experiences with my own book, *Around My World*. At the end I hoped I had persuaded him to do it. He had a great knack for expressing himself in an entertaining way and given his extensive travel experience there would be no shortage of stories.

A Most Improbable Adventure

After being a tourist in Granada the next morning, including breakfast at what was probably one of the most expensive restaurants in town, Kathy's Waffle House, and visits to the myriad churches in the city, including the beautiful, baroque Iglesia de La Merced and its famous bell tower, I was tired, hot, and in need of a break. I headed back to the hostel and had a relaxing dip in the pool. It cooled me off and slowed me down – exactly as it was meant to.

I hooked up with Christina and Phil in the afternoon for a stroll through Calle La Calzada – the main strip of tourist-friendly bars, shops, and restaurants that ran all the way to Lake Nicaragua – Central America's largest. I paid a handsome price for a small cup of chocolate ice cream that was absolutely delicious. We eventually stopped at a randomly selected bar so my new friends could slake their thirst with the nation's favourite beer, Toña.

We sat and chatted for a while as the sweat dripped down my back, chest, arms, legs and face. I felt like I had just stepped out of the shower – except my privates were covered. As a non-drinker I watched with a pinch of envy as they downed their cold beers with extreme pleasure.

As we talked I learned that Phil had been an information technology guru in a past life. He was in charge of dozens of software engineers that developed the latest and greatest features of mobile phones around the world.

"For eight years I worked with Nokia, three years in India, some in the U.K. and I even spent a few months in Vancouver. I was all over the place, really. I got pretty tired of working 80-hour weeks though," he said.

"And that's why you've been traveling for a year and a half," I jumped in. "I can see why you've chosen that path", I added.

"Yeah. They ask me back once in a while but I just can't do it."

"I don't blame you," I said. "You seem to have a pretty good life and you're enjoying yourself."

"Yeah, I like what I'm doing. I like to travel around and I like to learn Spanish. I want to settle down in a Latin American country eventually, I just haven't decided which one yet."

As we continued our stroll the sky quickly darkened and the winds picked up. The palm trees near the lake began to sway and bend. It looked like a dark cloak had been thrown over the lake and it was swiftly moving toward shore. The wind picked up even more speed and bent the palm fronds on the trees completely straight out, perpendicular to the ground, as though a giant hair dryer was blasting them at close range.

We passed by a beaten down old baseball diamond where young boys were playing. They looked to be maybe seven or eight years old. They pitched and hit and caught the ball with power and speed that defied their young age; it looked almost effortless. It all seemed very normal until I noticed an old white cow standing in center field, munching on the limited grass that was available. The boys kept on playing despite the wind, the impending rain, and the cow.

Right next to the baseball diamond was a basketball court, also very much worse for wear. Some teenagers, decked out in high-top shoes and NBA-style shorts and jerseys were playing a game. They, too, seemed rather indifferent to the wind, then strong enough to nearly cause me to lose my balance. I expected the sky to open up and dump on us at any moment.

As we passed through Calle La Calzada almost at a jog the rain began to lightly fall. As we walked it came down more strongly; enormous wet drops splattering the sidewalk and my sandaled feet. After all the build-up and extremely strong wind whipping in off the lake the rain was rather tame and lasted only a few minutes. We seemed to be the only ones concerned with it as everyone else just went about their business like they knew exactly what was going to happen, which, of course, they did.

For dinner that night I had something I almost never eat outside of North America – beef. Christina and Phil ordered

A Most Improbable Adventure

burgers and fries so I decided to be brave and do the same. It was awful of course but I managed to get most of it down and, more importantly, kept it down. It was Phil's last night in Granada so he wanted to go big. He was off to Costa Rica the next morning and then on to Panama.

"You have to let us know if you get picked up in a limo this time," I joked.

"Yeah, that would be something," Phil said with a smile.

"Maybe he lives in a massive mansion and you'll stay in the guest house and have a driver at your disposal," I continued.

"Well, apparently he's done quite well. I don't know about guest houses and drivers though."

"Based on your history, Phil, I wouldn't be at all surprised."

That night I sat on a comfortable seat in the common area of the hostel, reflecting on the past few days. I had again met someone with an amazing story about change and knowing what made them happy. Phil, tired of a hectic work life, had decided to leave the insanity behind and created something more meaningful for himself. He was roughly my age and chose an unpredictable path to fulfillment. He knew both what he wanted and what he did not want. He, too, was experiencing life through exploration. He was happy in the moment, not overly concerned about the next. As much as I may have inspired him to complete and publish his book he inspired me to consider what was truly important in life and live life in the moment. I suddenly had an image of Earl in my mind. He, too, was very present, not overly concerned with the past or future. I had to remind myself that Earl was gone. It jolted me back into my reality. I don't know how much time had passed but I felt tired so headed off to my uncomfortable bed.

I didn't know what to expect when I signed up for a kayak tour of Las Isletas the following day. I worried that there may not be enough people signed up to even go and the trip would be cancelled, like the volcano-boarding in Léon. Granada was painted over nicely to attract plenty of tourists and the infrastructure was in place for many, many more people than were currently there. My hostel was less than a quarter full, according to the young lady at the front desk. It was slow, to be sure.

As it turned out only Christina and I went on the kayak tour. All they needed was two people, and we were it. At least it wouldn't be crowded, other than the suffocating taxi ride to the lake on which we were joined by a lone Mexican man who was doing a lake tour by boat.

Our guide for the kayak tour, Miguel, did not look like what I expected a kayak guide to look like. I expected a taller, more muscular and masculine character, not a slightly pudgy, mildly effeminate individual that stood a shade over five feet tall. He gave us instructions on how to get into the kayaks without hurting ourselves – at least I guessed they were instructions. I made out only about one-third of what he said, but it was enough to know what to do to not eventually drift off into the lake and become dinner for the sharks.

The kayak I had was extremely short, especially given my height, so I spent most of my time paddling to keep the damn thing straight. The dense, dark, lake water provided nothing of an aquatic nature to look at and aside from a couple of birds and flowers there was little to see. There were, however, a couple of magnificent houses built on some of the Isletas, which were formed when nearby Volcán Mombacho erupted over 10,000 years ago. Perhaps the most beautiful of the properties was owned, I was told, by the man who owned, amongst other things, Toña beer. He apparently owned many properties around the world and thus rarely graced this particular abode with his presence.

Las Isletas are home to several hundred people living off the lake itself. They set fish traps for food and washed clothes and bathed in the lake. It reminded me very much of the backwaters of India; I felt like I was looking right into someone's living room as I floated past. As we slipped through the volcanic stones we spotted small huts and shacks that were fastened together by wood, rope, metal, and any other material that could be found. It was certainly less populated than India but it felt similar, especially when I saw many young children swimming and playing near their homes.

The open water of Lake Nicaragua, which covered an area over 8,000 square kilometres, was surprisingly rough. The wind whipped up meaningful waves that needed to be navigated carefully. Fresh water sharks, the only species of their kind in the world, were a real threat here, though unlikely to be present where we were going, I was told. The sharks, amazingly, had adapted to the fresh water over time as they were able to swim from the Caribbean up the San Juan River and into the lake.

On the return trip back to the dock I spotted two other kayakers heading our way. They didn't seem to have a guide, it was just two young men attempting to paddle their way through the many rocks that protrude through the lake's surface. Suddenly, one of them smacked into a rock and tumbled into the water, splashing about as if re-enacting a scene from *Jaws*.

Miguel quickly responded to the young man's aid. He diverted from his original direction and parked his kayak on the marshy shore nearest the man and jumped into the water – wearing jeans and a t-shirt. The lake was not deep at that point so he stood up and waded out to the half-sunk kayak. He dumped the water out and dragged it, and the man, to shore. After helping the man back into his vessel Miguel got back into his own and joined us, taking the lead for the last stretch across the choppy waters back to the dock.

That afternoon Christina and I decided that after our demonstration of athletic prowess on the water we deserved a nice coffee. We went to the Euro Café, adjacent to Parque Central.

"Let's grab a seat over there," she said as we entered the modest shop.

"Cool. Let's go take a look in the glass case at the front there and see what kind of treats they might have."

"Is it just me or do you like sweets?"

"Yeah, that's my weakness," I said with a smile.

As I pondered the various goods in the case the pretty young woman behind it spoke to me, in a soft and gentle voice: "They look good don't they?"

"They sure do. Do you work here?"

"Yes, my name is Caitlin."

"Nice to meet you, Caitlin, my name is Jason and this is my friend Christina. You don't sound like you are from here."

"No, I'm from the U.S., from Maryland."

"I'm from Canada and Christina here is from Denmark."

"Well, welcome to both of you. What can I get you?"

"Well, before you get me anything, can you tell me how a girl from Maryland ends up working at a coffee shop in Granada? Sorry, I have an inquiring mind."

"No problem. Well, I work and live here on the weekends. I live near Laguna de Apoyo during the week. My friends and I started a non-profit there called The Peace Project. We focus on peace education and English language instruction."

"Wow, that's amazing," Christina jumped in.

"I was about the say the exact same thing," I said, again deeply impressed with yet another young person on my trip that had done so much at such a young age. I didn't ask but she couldn't have been more than about twenty-four.

"It's no big deal," she said, shyly. "It's something I've wanted to do for a long time and I already knew how to speak Spanish so I finally took the plunge. It's incredibly rewarding but can be very difficult as well. If I didn't work here on the weekends the project wouldn't survive very long. We are always on the brink of having to shut things down."

"It takes a special person to do what you are doing. It's really impressive, the commitment you've made to it. You should be very proud," I gushed.

"Thank you both, you are very kind. Now, what can I get you?"

"Well, what do you recommend," I asked.

"That over there is our house special," she said, pointing to a turtle-shaped cookie.

"The one that looks like a turtle?"

"Yes, it's actually called, interestingly enough, the Turtle Cookie; it's our most popular one."

"Well, if you say so, I'll take two of those."

"I hope you enjoy them."

"I'm sure I will. You know, we were planning to go to Laguna de Apoyo tomorrow. I'm not sure if we'll be in the area of the Peace Project but if we are we'll stop by."

"That's great. I hope you can make it. If not, that's okay too. It was nice meeting you both."

"You too," Christina and I said, almost in unison.

The Turtle Cookie, shortbread with dark chocolate and caramel drizzled on top of shaved nuts, turned out to be spectacular. For a mere dollar I was in heaven, if only for a brief moment. I had found that my sweet tooth was on extra high alert over the past few weeks given the somewhat bland offerings throughout Central America and this definitely hit the spot.

That evening I went a step further and splurged on a magnificent Mahi Mahi dinner at Imagine, an upscale restaurant owned by an American named Kevin. Kevin's friend Jeremy, who hailed from California, was running the place that particular night. He'd been working like a dog in the U.S. and decided to move to Nicaragua and help his friend instead. Escaping hectic lives elsewhere seemed to be a common theme in many of the conversations I had had to that point in my trip.

Having spent the equivalent of only a few dollars on most of meals for several weeks it felt odd, and even a little unsettling, to pay North American prices for a meal but the fish and locally harvested vegetables were so savoury it just didn't matter. I was initially intrigued by Imagine because it was known for a famous dessert – mango bread. It was available by the slice or in a giant mound of sugary goodness – so I of course chose the latter. Three large chunks of warm mango bread were topped with a heap of vanilla ice cream and drizzled with Ghirardelli chocolate. To say it was decadent would be sadly insufficient. I had spent more on that meal than I had spent on nearly every night of accommodation on the trip, but I had lost the ability to care.

I expected the shuttle to Laguna de Apoyo the next day to be full. Apoyo was described in every travel guide as an idyllic lake, nearly perfectly round as it was formed in the crater of a volcano. Only two others showed up for the short ride however: Christina and Lindsay – a woman staying at the same hostel.

"Where are you from?" I inquired.

"I'm from New York but I've been living in Costa Rica for the past five years," Lindsay replied.

"Oh, really? Where in Costa Rica?"

"In a little beach town called Samara. I'm actually in Nicaragua doing a visa run. I need to be out for seventy-two hours so I can get another ninety days in the country."

"I need to do the opposite run in the next few days," Christina offered. "I need to go to Costa Rica for a few days to get a new ninety days as well. I'm going to be staying in León for the next few months."

"Yeah, I've done lots of those runs in the past five years."

"So, what do you do in Samara?" I asked.

"I'm a yoga instructor and I also sing, mostly at weddings. That's right, I'm an actual wedding singer," she said with a broad smile.

"Are there a lot of Americans who come down for destination weddings?" I asked.

"Yes, lots. It's surprising really. And they spend ridiculous amounts of money to do it. I make enough doing one wedding; singing for a couple of hours, to pay a month's rent."

"Is that a function of low rent, too?"

A Most Improbable Adventure

"Yeah, it's rather cheap there. I live right on the beach. Everything else is expensive though, basically American prices."

The conversation was non-stop for the thirty-minute ride to Apoyo as the three of us exchanged questions and answers. It's the nature of traveling, really; a lot of time spent sharing details of personal situations and stories. From that I could place people into nice, neat little compartments in my mind. It was a way to remember times and places in an otherwise jumbled mass of trip-related memories. Some of these interactions became memorable and thinking of a place in the future reminded me of the person or people I met, not unlike how certain smells and sounds remind us of certain times in our lives.

We arrived at the sister property of the hostel we were staying at in Granada and the driver informed us he would be back in the afternoon to pick us up. The gate suddenly opened up and a tall red-headed girl greeted us. "Hola, and welcome!"

I didn't catch her name but I caught the other demographic data: twenty-three year old, from California. She walked us through the grounds pointing out where everything was. She spoke with a soft, gentle, yet inviting voice.

"You're free to go wherever you want, including down the road to town, but everything you need is here," she said. I felt like I had just entered a commune.

I sat in a swinging chair overlooking the lake for the next two hours, writing, thinking, and reflecting. Christina and Lindsay did much the same, lounging and relaxing in the serenity of it all. As I sat I thought back to the big, dirty, smelly cities like Mexico City, Guatemala City, San Salvador, and Managua and was thankful to be in such a serene and quiet place. My mind tended to slow down at times like this and I felt more connected to nature in some way.

At lunch we found a tiny shop just up the road that served the standard chicken, rice, and beans I had then become accustomed to, and tired of, and sat on an outdoor patio. It was there that Lindsay spoke of her lack of desire to return to the U.S.

"It's such a mess there. Nothing seems to be working. And during an election campaign it is impossible to hear about anything else. In Costa Rica I don't even think about the economy, politics, crime, and all the mass information that is pushed on people in the States. Ignorance is truly blissful, especially if you are from the States."

I chuckled a little at her last comment but it really did make sense. In Costa Rica she would not be exposed to the stupidity of goings on in her native land.

"You know," Lindsay broke my train of thought, "I don't even like the name of my country. United States of America makes no sense. Everything from Canada down to the tip of Chile is really America. And then there are other United States too, like Mexico – Estados Unidos de Mexico. It just doesn't make sense."

Lindsay was not like some Americans, who may have limited understanding of, and little interest in, what happened outside their borders. Lindsay was educated, spoke Spanish, and was integrated into her community through her business and through volunteering. She was young, vibrant, and made the conscious choice to re-locate to a place in the world that resonated more with her. She was centred, and very aware of what she was doing and how she wanted to live her life. Given that I didn't even really know her I felt oddly proud of her for living her life in such a way. The world needed more people to live that way.

Later that afternoon, back in Granada, the three of us casually walked along Calle La Calzada in search of fancy coffees. We found a beautiful courtyard next to which such coffees were served. We sat, relaxing in the comfort of the flower-laden courtyard listening to the fountain dribble water over its edges. I loved my coffee moments and this was one of them.

"I love the way some of these English menus read," I said with a chuckle. "Look here, it says "with" but it's spelled w-h-i-t and mocha is spelled m-o-h-c-a in one place and m-o-c-h-h-a in another. I love that." I suddenly felt like an idiot, pointing these things out. It's not like my Spanish was great. Besides, what kind of thing is that to say, anyway?

"I know," Lindsay jumped in. "You'd think they would have someone proofread these things. They clearly cater to tourists and offer menus in English, why don't they proofread? I should take a picture of this menu, it's full of mistakes."

"You take pictures of menus with spelling errors?" I asked.

"Yeah, I kind of have a thing for that."

"That's okay," I offered. I take pictures of signs that show you what you are not allowed to do. You know, no parking, smoking, pissing on the grass, that kind of thing."

"I was thinking of doing a coffee table book with misspelled words from menus," she said.

"That's a great idea," I laughed.

The three of us continued to chat like old high school friends. It was then that Christina explained the Danish language and other interesting tidbits about Denmark.

"Danish is very similar to Norwegian and Norwegian is very similar to Swedish but Danish and Swedish are not at all alike."

"What?" I said. "That doesn't make much sense."

"I know, it's complicated," she said.

She went on to further explain that Dutch was really German and English smashed together and Finnish was closer to Russian. It was all very enlightening, as was the fact that Denmark was once much larger than it is today – once encompassing Norway, Iceland, and parts of Germany. If I hadn't been thrown in that Granada-bound bus in Managua a few days prior I doubt I would have ever learned so much about Denmark.

In the centre of the main market in Granada is the bus "station" – really just an empty patch of dirt with a half-dozen broken down chicken buses idling and belching smoke into the already thick air. It was here that Christina and I found the bus to the city of Rivas. Someone immediately grabbed our backpacks and threw them up on top of the bus where sacks of fruits, nuts, and other packages were crammed together. Images immediately came to mind of my backpack flying off at some point on the road, never to be seen again. It was out of my hands now so there was nothing I could do but hope it made it to our destination.

It was sweltering hot in the bus and perspiration dripped off my forehead and arms as I tried to get settled in. I could see beads of sweat gather on every inch of my exposed skin. Thankfully the bus rolled away only a few minutes later – generating a slight breeze through the window that provided some level of relief.

As with all chicken buses in Central America it stopped frequently to let people off and collect new passengers. There were no actual bus stops just random spots on the road where people somehow knew to be and when. Thus, a fairly short distance took several hours for the bus to cover.

At one point, the bus already packed with people sitting and standing, a man came aboard carrying a bible. He instantly began yelling at the top of his lungs about the virtues of the Lord. He wore some form of identity badge around his neck, on which I could just make out a word that I assumed translated to "Evangelical." He proceeded to scream for about the next twenty minutes while everyone ignored him and avoided eye contact.

Shortly after the preacher stopped berating us another man boarded the bus with something to say. He was a salesman, pushing some sort of candy product. He, too, yelled for quite some time and then, mercifully, shut up. He was replaced at the next stop by yet another man, this one was part-salesman, part-preacher. He was informing all on board about the virtues of learning how to speak English. His bible was a pamphlet

A Most Improbable Adventure

that offered English courses, his teachers being the best around, naturally. His diatribe, also yelled at the top of his lungs, only lasted about five minutes before he stepped off at the next stop. That's not something I see every day on the subway in Toronto, I thought.

As we exited the bus at Rivas we were immediately attacked by taxi drivers offering to take us to San Jorge, where we would take a ferry to Ometepe Island. I was grabbed on each arm by two different men screaming at me "Taxi, Taxi, Taxi to San Jorge!" Christina was also attacked and nearly knocked over in the mayhem. A young couple, clearly tourists, had arrived in Rivas at the same time and were trying to fight their way through the swarm of waving arms as well. Christina managed to make her way to the other woman and asked where they were going and what they were planning to do. The taxi drivers then all left me alone and swarmed around the two women who were nearly screaming to be able to hear each other. The other woman, clearly fed up with being pawed, thrust her arms out to create some space and yelled "Uno momento séniores!" With that they finally backed off.

It turned out that there were four of them, from Germany, and they were trying to get a taxi for four. Christina and I then got a $10 taxi, negotiated down to $4. Once inside the car the noise abated and I was able to think and breathe again. The odour in the car—once enough to nearly knock me out—no longer concerned me as I had since become accustomed to it and my only concern at that point was getting to our destination, rather than deciding which window to vomit out of.

As we stepped out of the taxi at the ferry terminal we were immediately accosted by a man wearing some form of official-looking identity badge around his neck. He spoke perfect English and kindly informed us of the departure times and destinations for the boats but also tried to convince us to stay at a particular hotel and sign up for a tour right there on the spot. I brushed him off and swiftly walked past him.

At the end of the dock was a large ferry capable of carrying a number of vehicles and had several levels for passengers. I hoped that it would be our ride because the other options were tiny wooden vessels that had clearly seen better days. Christina, with her excellent command of what she called "Travel Spanish" deduced that, in fact, we were not going on the big ferry but were, instead, going on the smallest boat moored there, a craft I swiftly dubbed "The Deathtrap."

"I'm definitely going to take a Gravol before I get on that thing," I said.

"It looks awfully small," Christina noted, not making me feel any better.

"The travel guidebooks all say to take a morning ferry because the waves in the afternoon can be very choppy and here we are in the middle of the afternoon," I said, with a sense of doom.

"Hopefully it won't be that bad," she said, smiling meekly, hopefully.

"Did you look closely at that thing? It's made of wood and there are tons of holes and patches all over it. Holy shit."

"True, it looks a little beat up."

I stood there, looking at it, hoping that the passage of a few minutes would somehow make the situation better. Finally, reluctantly, we crossed the plank and got on board. Over the next few minutes only a half-dozen or so other souls were brave enough to come aboard. Several extremely rough looking men then came aboard, opened up the hatch in the floor and began loading supplies into the hull. Bags of rice, fruit, and even household appliances came on and into the hold below. Ballast, perhaps? A man then came around with a clipboard in his hand. We were to write our name, age, and nationality on the paper. It was the official record of our being aboard that day, I concluded.

"I guess this is what they'll use to figure out which embassy to call when the ship sinks," I said, mostly joking.

"We'll be fine. No problem," Christina said, again with hope rather than confidence in her voice.

"I guess we'll find out."

After the final supplies were loaded the boat slowly began to pull away from the dock. I had a flashback to Lake Titicaca in Bolivia, on which I sat aboard an equally questionable vessel as it ever-so-slowly slogged through the water and miraculously deposited me at my destination unscathed. The Deathtrap seemed to move at the same unbearably slow pace. I referred to a small pamphlet the clipboard man had handed me; it was a brief and horribly written promotional flyer referring to the fact that the boat was the only wooden construction vessel still plying the waters of Lake Nicaragua. It was powered by a 350-hp engine, measured 19-metres in length and dated from the early 1980s. I quickly figured out why it was moving so slowly. That kind of horsepower is only meaningful if the engine is in a car. In a boat that size it was no wonder we moved at a snail's pace – especially against the choppy waves that relentlessly hit us head-on.

Ometepe is only about twenty kilometres from San Jorge but it had taken over two hours to get there. We encountered exactly zero minutes of smooth sailing. It rocked and bounced and splashed every, single, possible, second. On several occasions we were soaked by enormous sprays of water, much to the delight of other passengers, who were wise to sit away from the outside edges of the boat.

Just to make me feel better about The Deathtrap, every ten minutes or so a crew member appeared to start hand-pumping water out of the belly of the boat, working furiously for several minutes before breaking and then starting again. He pulled on what appeared to be a broom handle, which was inserted into a narrow pipe that was inserted into the floor. As he pulled on the handle the water below was siphoned up and out of a hose, draining along the deck to a small hole on the side and back out to the lake. Nearly every stroke he made brought up more water than the pipe could handle so the deck was constantly splashed and soaked with water.

As the boat heaved and pounded against the waves the force of impact sent shimmers through the wooden hull, vibrating my spine and brain inside my skull. I was happy to have taken the Gravol before leaving because there were plenty of occasions when the starboard side of the deck was only inches above the water's surface one moment and the next moment I was looking up at the sky as the boat heaved back.

When we finally arrived I stepped on dry land and felt a sort of thrill for having survived the journey, as though I had cheated certain death. My moment of exhilaration was shattered by the all-too-familiar shouts of "Taxi, Taxi, Taxi!" I knew my hotel was not very far but after having survived the trip across the lake I wasn't in the mood to slog my backpack an undetermined distance in the late afternoon heat so I got a taxi from perhaps the sleaziest looking man I had ever encountered. He was of medium height and build with a dark complexion and black hair slicked back extremely tightly on his tiny little head.

"I'm a professional tour guide, where would you like to go? We can do a tour right now, okay?" he said, not allowing me an opportunity to speak.

It was all I could do to stop myself from punching him in the face. As an alternative I simply informed him that I'd just arrived and all I wanted to do was get to my hotel and relax.

"No problem," he replied. "Maybe tomorrow?"

"Maybe tomorrow," I said, having no intention to call him, ever. I just wanted him to stop talking – immediately.

As we rolled up to the hotel I noticed it looked rather deserted. Sleazy man jumped out to show me where the front desk was, which was rather obviously right in front of me. A young man appeared and asked if he could help. I asked if he had any rooms and he said he did, though he looked rather stunned and unsure. Sleazy man started bothering him too, asking for a commission for bringing me to the hotel, even though I told him that's where I wanted to go. The boy was having nothing of sleazy man's bullshit but he kept hanging around for several more minutes. Finally, after lounging around for an uncomfortably long time, he left.

At a hotel that I estimated could host about a hundred people there were exactly fourteen at breakfast the next day, including a ten-member Nicaraguan family. Hence there were no takers for a guided tour being offered by a pleasant-looking young man at one of the tables. No takers except Christina and me of course. The guide, whose name was Will (the same as my then 8-month old son), informed us that because there were only two of us we wouldn't be taking the comfortable tourist van around the island; we'd be taking the local chicken buses. Low season had bitten once again.

Will was in his early thirties with a slight build, deep brown eyes, and a very gentle presence. He had studied English in the United States on a refugee visa because he was considered a politically persecuted individual during the Nicaraguan civil war. His father had been killed during the war, though he didn't mention where on the political spectrum his loyalties lay – not that it mattered. He had incredibly energy and was knowledgeable in biology, archeology, and perhaps a few other things that ended in "ology." Right from the beginning it didn't feel like a tour; it felt like I was hanging out with a local friend who happened to know a whole bunch of stuff about a whole bunch of things.

"Hurry, let's run! The bus is already there!" he shouted.

The bus rattled along the road in front of us as we emerged from the lane that led to the hotel. The bus had clearly seen better days.

"We'll take this bus to Altagracia to the see the church and the pre-Columbian artifacts," he said.

"Is that the church with the vampire bats?" Christina asked.

"Yes, that's the one," he replied.

Taking a hotel near San Juan rather than Altagracia looked like a better and better decision as the streets of Altagracia rolled by. It was simply an ugly city, period. Its central park was uninspiring and the area around it was run-down and neglected.

Will then showed us inside the nearly 100-year-old cathedral that boasted hundreds of vampire bats hanging upside down behind the altar. The stench of bat piss on the walls and floor made for a quick visit. There was little of note inside or around it, save for the so-called pre-Columbian statues situated in its courtyard. Outside of the church, near the central park, I spotted the sleazy tour guide from the day before, trying to hustle two tourists who clearly wanted nothing to do with him.

The hike to the lookout point near El Porvenir didn't seem particularly daunting in concept. It was to be only a couple of hours of hiking. Unfortunately, because we had been taking public transit, we were delayed in arriving and therefore slogged up a rugged and rocky path in the heat of the day – and it was hot. I'm certain I lost several pounds of sweat on the way up.

Along the way we met farmers harvesting rice – not something I expected to see on an island in Lake Nicaragua, at altitude no less.

"It's genetically modified rice, more hardy than you would find in Asia," Will commented, likely seeing the perplexed look on my face. The rice fields sprawled out along the hillside, growing green and tall in and amongst the black volcanic boulders.

"How do they plant this here, with rocks everywhere?" I asked.

"Usually they use a stick and hit the ground like this," he said, as he drove a tree branch vertically into the soil. "It creates a small hole. Then usually an old woman or small child would come along behind and drop the seed in the hole and cover it up. That's the way they have to do it here. There is no room for large mechanical equipment up here and because of the rock they can't use conventional methods."

"That sounds like extremely hard work," I said, perhaps stating the obvious.

"It is very, very hard work," he replied.

As I looked up across the hillside I still couldn't quite believe that I was looking at rice fields – it just didn't seem to conceptually fit in my mind. Amongst the rice were volcanic rock, some enormous boulders over ten feet high, as well as stands of large mature trees and other fields that had been burned to enrich the soil for the following year's crops. And it all somehow hung together on the side of a rising volcano.

At the lookout point I stopped to catch my breath, sweat pouring out of me. I turned to see what I had gone there to see – a vista that included Volcán Concepción and Volcán Máderas, the shorter of the two volcanoes that make up Ometepe, and on which we stood. The lake stretched out as far as the eye could see to the East and the spinning wind generators on the mainland to the West. Despite the altitude the air was warm and the sun blazing hot.

After a late lunch we walked down that part of the island's main road – there were no buses in sight. In fact, there was hardly any traffic at all – only an occasional motorbike, or random horse or cow. We walked several kilometres until Will flagged down a large watermelon truck.

"Come on, they'll give us a ride!" he yelled.

Once again we ran as fast as we could toward the back of a huge, open-top truck. A dark hand and arm reached down and pulled me up to the deck several feet off the pavement. The truck was empty but had palm and other leaves draped over the edges of its perimeter. They were, Will informed me, for padding when carrying fruits, like watermelons so they wouldn't get bruised or damaged during transit.

I only had time to grab onto a bar to brace myself before the truck jerked forward, nearly sending me flat on my face.

As the truck sped down the road the lower branches of passing trees nearly whacked me in the head.

"Duck!" yelled Will.

I did so just in time as a thick branch whizzed by my head. The man standing in front of me then became the signal for when I needed to crouch down. Every time he ducked I did so a fraction of a second later. My white knuckles got rapped a few times but my head stayed on for the next ten minutes as we lumbered down the road.

"That was pretty close," Christina said as we disembarked the truck.

"Yeah, that was. Just imagine; if we had been a bigger group we would have traveled in a comfortable tourist shuttle bus, not in the back of a watermelon truck!"

Our next stop was the thermal springs, situated on someone's private property. After a short walk through a pasture we reached the thermal pool. In my experience a thermal pool was a naturally occurring pool of water rising up from the ground that was always warm, sometimes even very hot – hence the term hot springs. This pool, however, was something rather short of hot. Fortunately, it felt extremely refreshing as my body had been near to overheating the entire day. After a quick dip all was right with the world.

The sun was setting as I changed back into my walking shorts in the small outside stall. Within minutes it was almost completely dark, causing me to stumble as I stepped out of the stall and down the stone path toward the exit. I met Christina and Will and we headed out to the main road through the woods just as the sun hit the horizon. I turned to look back into the sky and saw a huge sweeping cloud above, like a mushroom cap covering the hills in the distance. In a moment the sky was black. We hit the main road, dimly lit by the appearing moon.

"How far away are we from the hotel?" I inquired.

"A few kilometres," Will replied with a look on his face that said it was quite a few kilometres. "Maybe we can catch a ride again," he added.

A Most Improbable Adventure

For the next fifteen minutes we walked in silence in the pitch darkness. Not a single vehicle or beast came down the road in either direction. Had I not been with Will I would have surely been more concerned.

"I've hitched all over the island for many years," he said, breaking the silence. "Not to worry, we'll get a ride soon. Somebody always shows up. It's not usually this quiet. I know many people from around here; somebody is bound to drive by."

As though he had just rubbed a magic lantern at that moment the sound of a rumbling engine could be heard in the distance; it was deafening in the silence. Just then Will stepped into the middle of the road. Lights appeared around the corner and he began waving his arms. The oncoming vehicle slowed and pulled alongside us. It was a tourist-style shuttle van with a passenger up front. Will quickly approached it and with lightning speed had negotiated us a ride for the equivalent of about a dollar each. I happily paid it and hopped into the back. After more than fifteen minutes of driving we finally arrived back at the hotel – meaning if we had walked it would have taken us a couple of hours or more. I was glad to be back, to be in one piece, and to be in good spirits after a day of exploring Ometepe in one of the most unusual ways I could have conceived.

The next day was a travel day. I'm always wary of travel days that require changing modes of transportation. Traveling from Ometepe Island to Liberia, Costa Rica should not be daunting, I thought; it was only about 150 kilometres away after all. That said it would require more than one taxi, a ferry, and more than one bus – a lot of changing, switching, and dealing with people yelling in my face.

Getting to the ferry was easy enough, just a short ride from the hotel. As we turned to go down the road to the launch I thought about the death trap that brought us there.

"I hope the ride back will be on a big ferry, not that crappy little box of firewood we came here in," I said to Christina.

"I'm sure it won't be the death trap," she said, trying to sound positive.

I let out an audible sigh of relief as the ferry came into view – the largest one I had seen on the lake. It was being loaded with large trucks carrying fruit and other supplies. I was pleased to know we'd made such an upgrade versus the trip there.

Onboard there were only a handful of people, including only one other tourist. Her name was Kate and she worked for an NGO based in Baltimore, Maryland. She had been at a conference in Managua and decided to do a quick excursion to Ometepe before heading home.

"I had a couple of days so I thought I would come here and check it out. It's a nice little island, and very quiet."

"Yeah, it's incredibly slow right now; hardly any tourists anywhere," I added.

"How long have you been traveling?"

"About a month. I go home to Canada in a week or so."

"And how about you?" she said, looking at Christina.

"I'm about five months into a year of traveling through Central and South America."

"Wow, where are you from?"

"I'm from Denmark," Christina replied.

"And what are you traveling for?" Kate asked me.

"Well, I'm an author and travel writer. I have a wife and two young boys at home so I'm not going to be away for a year like some people I know," I said as I smiled at Christina.

"How old are your sons?"

"Sam is three-and-a-half and Will is eight months."

"Wow, eight months! And your wife let you go to Central America for over a month?"

"Yeah, she's pretty awesome. Of course, she didn't really *let* me go. It was her idea."

"Her idea! Wow, that's so great. I bet you miss your kids."

"Oh, boy, do I ever. I can't wait to see them."

"Do you have kids, Christina?"

"No, it's just me," she replied.

"Me too," Kate offered. I travel a fair bit all over the world because of my work, so…"

Kate went on to tell about the various places she had been for her development work and Christina and I shared our various travel stories, acquired over many years. Before I knew it the very smooth ride across to the mainland was complete.

Rather than endure the hassle of getting a bus—which one and when, I had no idea—to the Costa Rican border we decided to take a taxi. It was surely more expensive but we'd be there quicker in greater comfort and I was all in favour of such a plan.

I had read that the border crossing at Peñas Blancas was extremely confusing. Nothing was clearly marked and there was about a kilometre of no-man's land between exiting Nicaragua and entering Costa Rica. Because of this a number of touts were known to approach travelers making the journey and tell them that they could help navigate the maze and complete the paperwork for them – for a fee, of course. Knowing this I steeled myself as I exited the taxi. I had not put my second foot on the ground when the cacophony began.

"Official form! I help you! Official form!" the screaming began.

"After I had said "No, gracias" to the third or fourth person I thought I had made it into the clear. I was wrong. Another man jumped in my path and pointed to a turnstile – implying I needed to pass through it. I readied my passport and showed it to the official looking man in the white shirt. He glanced at it, asked for a dollar, and showed me through.

One of the touts followed me through the turnstile and said loudly, unnecessarily so as he was literally in my back pocket, "Where are you going? Official form! I can help you!" Christina was right behind him.

I ignored him and kept walking toward an official looking building. I didn't know if it was the right building but it wasn't, like most, in complete ruins. I did not allow myself to look away from my target, not drifting in my attention. I had hoped that if I kept my focus going forward he's leave me alone. I thought I had just exited Nicaragua and now needed to find the right place to enter Costa Rica. The tout continued to follow me at an unacceptable distance as I flailed about, not sure where to go.

"This way!" he shouted, pointing toward one of several buildings, any one of which could have been the correct one. Having no other idea where the hell to go I took his advice. Up ahead I saw the two Germans I had seen in San Jorge.

"Where are you guys going?" I asked.

"We're going to Monteverde," the young woman replied. "How about you?"

"Liberia. Is that Tica Bus person over there trying to sell you a ride?"

"Yes, but we're not sure what we're going to do." "We're going to catch a local bus, I think."

"Well, good luck."

"Yes, you too."

I then approached a kiosk where I was asked for another two dollars and told to fill out a form – the official form the tout had been shoving in my face the whole time. I thought I had already left Nicaragua and was about to ask why I had to pay again – and then I thought better of it. The tout hung on my shoulder just a bit too long, so I turned and said a few harsh words that I would not repeat in front of my children – finally forcing him to release his near death-grip on me. He scurried away like a dog that had been kicked in the ass. I felt relieved, like I had killed an annoying mosquito that had been dive-bombing me all day.

We made our way to yet another kiosk where another person was looking at passports. This particular guy was wearing jeans and a golf shirt with the Costa Rican emblem on it. I figured we were in Costa Rica by that point but again I was wrong. Christina approached a nearby police officer and asked where we should go as the previous guy had not stamped our passports. He instructed her, after an extremely long evaluation of her passport, to keep going to the building ahead.

We kept walking and eventually came to a building with a long line-up in front of it in the form of a snaking queue and a massive gate with a small man regulating the flow of people through it.

"*This* must be where we finally enter Costa Rica," I said, hoping I was right.

"This looks more official. How many times did we show our passports, five or six times?" Christina said.

"Way too many. That was crazy."

"This no-man's land is ridiculous."

"Hey, did you ever buy that onward ticket out of Costa Rica or are you going to buy a voucher?" I asked her.

"I didn't buy anything. Everything I've read said that the likelihood of being asked for that is pretty small."

"Let's hope so."

We stood stationary for about fifteen minutes as the sweat poured down my back. The little man hadn't let anyone through and it was not clear what he was waiting for. Just then he stepped aside and several of us plowed through the opening in the gate like cattle and through the door to the immigration checkpoint. Right away I noticed a sign that said each person entering Costa Rica must have proof of onward or return passage otherwise they would be denied entry. I pointed the sign out to Christina.

"Why don't you go first, since you have proof of a flight out of Panama City and I'll go right behind you?" she said. "Maybe he'll assume we're together and not ask for anything."

"Sounds good," I said. "I feel like an international spy suddenly." I didn't think it would work of course. If the guy was paying attention he'd certainly ask some questions. I had a Canadian passport and she had a Danish passport – that should have been his first clue. I had a wedding ring on, she didn't. Our passports would have stamps for entrances and exits that would show we weren't together. How could it possibly work?

"Passport, please," said the agent, his brows furrowed and forehead crumpled.

I handed it to him slowly. I then slipped him the printout of my flight itinerary from Panama City to Toronto. He examined it for a minute.

"You're leaving Panama City on October fourth?" he asked.

"Yes," I replied.

"He shuffled a few papers and then flicked his finger to send me on my way. I stepped aside and Christina stepped forward.

"Same flight as him?" he asked her.

"Yes," she lied.

"Go ahead."

Somehow her scheme had worked. She would not have to buy a ticket back to Nicaragua until she wanted, which was only going to be seventy-two hours anyway as she was only leaving Nicaragua in order to get a new ninety-day visa upon entry. We were on our way.

I wasn't going to a five-star beachside resort in Costa Rica, the typical destination for tourists. What might I encounter there? *Who* might I encounter?

JUST DON'T KILL ME

Upon arrival in Liberia I quickly picked up on one of the most obvious differences between Nicaragua and Costa Rica: the price of nearly everything more than quadrupled. A bottle of water that was fifty cents had suddenly become two dollars; a one-dollar taxi ride had become five dollars and a filling two-dollar lunch had become an unsatisfying nine-dollar lunch. It was an unpleasant shock.

We went to Café Liberia for dinner. The owner of the place, a Frenchman, came to chat with us for a few minutes. His accent was rather strong but I made out that the mushroom risotto was the special tonight. Having had less than stellar meals for quite some time, the risotto appealed to me, so I ordered it. In the end the meal was painfully expensive but the risotto was amazing.

The following day was another travel day. After asking a few different people what my best approach should be to get to Monteverde it seemed it was going to be an uncoordinated three-bus extravaganza – something I was not at all interested in. The alternative was to pay a huge sum of money to get a direct shuttle – a much more appealing option. I chose the latter option, only to find that there was not another soul in all of Liberia who wanted to go to Monteverde on the shuttle that day, crushing my plans. I was, yet again, the only person who wanted to do something and therefore the shuttle did not go.

As Christina was just waiting out her seventy-two hours she planned to stay in Liberia and I was moving on. As we walked to the bus station (she had the map) we passed the terminal for one of the branded coach companies. I decided to go in and check it out – desperate, really, for another option to get to Monteverde. The large board outside the ticket booth seemed to indicate that the schedule consisted of one route: Liberia to San José and San José to Liberia.

"Shit!" I said, disappointed.

"Let me ask," Christina offered.

After what seemed a long and drawn out conversation with the young man behind the glass she returned to tell me that none of the coach buses went to Monteverde, but there may be an alternative. It was a two-bus journey, the first dropping me off at a place that wasn't on either of my Costa Rica maps. The second bus, it was assumed, would come along and take me the rest of the way.

"That sounds like a solid plan," I said, about as sarcastically I could. "I've got a couple of real winning choices here, don't I?"

Just then a man approached Christina and started talking to her. He was a taxi driver, of course. Normally I would have ignored him but the idea of taking a taxi rather than two or three buses was an appealing one.

His first price was $100 US. I nearly choked. "I don't think so," I said, shaking my head.

His next offer was $50 to go to Tilarán, where I would catch the last bus to Monteverde. After some deliberation and negotiation I paid him $32 for what was ultimately an eighty-kilometre ride. A good deal in North America; an insane amount otherwise, though it had to be done. To top it off, he didn't even seem like an actual taxi driver. He drove a plain car – no taxi credentials whatsoever. I was about to get into the car of a random man hanging around the bus terminal. I discreetly took a piece of paper from a notepad in my bag and scribbled down the licence plate number and slipped it to Christina.

"I'll message you when I get to Tilarán to let you know I'm still alive."

"Great idea. Have a good trip," she said.

"You too. Thank you for everything."

"Thank you, too. Take care."

I then stepped into the back seat of his little car and hoped that he wasn't going to try to rip me off, or drive to some secluded location and slit my throat.

"Como te llamas?" he blurted out.

"Jason," I replied.

"*Jahsenn*," he repeated.

"J-a-s-o-n, si," I repeated, spelling it for him, letter by letter, in Spanish.

"Ah, Jason. Con mucho gusto."

"Como te llamas?" I asked.

"Manny," he replied.

"Bueno, Manny." *Just don't kill me.*

After driving only a few minutes he turned back to me and said, more or less, I deciphered, if the police stop us we are actually friends and I am not paying him anything for the ride.

"Bueno," I replied, indicating that I understood his devious little scheme.

The road to Cañas and then Tilarán was smooth and traffic was light. Manny and I didn't say a word and that was fine by me, and by him too it seemed. I was comfortable and rather pleased that I would be in Tilarán while it was still early in the morning. In fact, I was plenty early for the 12:30 bus to Monteverde so Manny decided he would hang out with me for a while – it seemed he was not, after all, a tourist-killing maniac.

Knowing it would take four hours to get to Monteverde despite it being only thirty-eight kilometres away I popped a couple of Gravol pills to fend off what would surely be a massive bout of nausea.

As the bus turned off the pavement onto the rutted, rock-riddled path I knew immediately why it would take four hours to get there. For the first two kilometres the bus was imprisoned in first gear. I could feel the wheels as they crawled over each and every rock, straining to move forward up the increasingly steep hill. One hairpin corner turned into another which turned into another – I was disoriented within minutes.

Eventually the Pacific Ocean came into view in the far off distance. It surprised me when I saw it – not thinking I'd be able to see it at such a distance. I wanted to savour the moment but unfortunately the bus jerked around yet another corner and nearly snapped my neck as the gorgeous view was ripped away.

I must have somehow nodded off for a while as I was surprised to see a sign that indicated Santa Elena was only twenty-four kilometres away. Had we stayed at the same pace as the first couple of kilometres of the trip I would very likely still be on that bus.

After twenty-four more grueling kilometres the bus finally jerked to a heaving halt. I stepped out with a smile on my face, again happy to not be moving and to have my feet planted solidly on the ground. I was immediately accosted by taxi drivers, which seemed odd given that most of the hostels in town were only a short walk from each other and from the town centre. I waved them off and started walking. I quickly found the turnoff for the hostel I had hoped to stay at—I hadn't pre-booked accommodations— and I lugged my backpack up and down yet another hilly, rock-strewn road. As I stepped into the reception area of the hostel I was greeted by the smiling face of José, who bore a striking resemblance to the actor Jeff Goldblum from the 1980s movie *The Fly*. Within minutes I had a place to rest my weary bones.

A Most Improbable Adventure

After settling into my room I headed back to ask José the most critical question I could conceive of at that moment: "Where can I get a good coffee around here?"

Without even blinking José reached for a stack of business cards on his desk, picked one up, handed it to me, and said, "The Common Cup. It's just down the road."

"Excelente. Muchas gracias," I replied

"If you go, tell Heynor that I sent you, but don't tell him José sent you, say Flaco sent you, nobody calls me José."

"Flaco? What does Flaco mean?"

"Skinny."

"That makes sense. I guess you could call me Flaco, too?

"Yes, I suppose so."

"I'll tell him Flaco sent me, for sure, thanks."

Just then a woman appeared in the reception area, someone I had seen only a few minutes prior as I dragged my backpack to my room. She had been sitting in one of the common areas of the hostel, relaxing with a book. We started chatting. I mentioned I was going for a coffee and asked if she would be interested in coming along. She agreed and off we went.

"I'm Donna by the way. I'm from England," she said as we walked.

"I'm Jason. It's nice to meet you."

Donna and I had one characteristic in common, I learned, that was different relative to the others in the hostel – we were close to forty, her on one side of it, me on the bad side.

"How long have you been traveling?" I asked.

"Just two weeks, how about you?" she replied.

"About a month. I started in Mexico City and I'm making my way to Panama City."

"I've been in Costa Rica so far but I'm planning to travel about ten months altogether."

"Wow, ten months. That's a long time, and you're only two weeks into it. That's very exciting," I said enthusiastically.

"Yeah, it's a bit daunting though. I've never really traveled like this before. In fact, I hadn't stayed in a hostel before two weeks ago."

"Really? You're a bit of a rookie then?"

"Yeah, I've been traveling with that guy you saw at the computer earlier. His name is Stijn; he's from Holland. I met him straight away at the airport in San José. It's funny actually. My hostel was supposed to have a pick-up for me at the airport but nobody showed up. I met Stijn and his friend and after a few minutes of talking we decided to work together, like a traveling team."

"That's a great idea. It can be hard to travel alone, especially when you've never really done anything like that before. Do you speak any Spanish?"

"No. I'm dreadful. Bloody awful, really. Stijn speaks it quite well; he's been my saviour."

"I know exactly what you mean. I've had my share of angels in my traveling life. It's great when you can work as a team and when they can help with the language it's a real bonus."

"That's for sure. I feel really lucky that it has worked out this way."

We then arrived at the coffee shop and I placed my order. "So what do you plan to do with your ten months? Actually, before you get to that, what do you do back in England?" I inquired.

"I'm a special needs teacher. I was able to get a year sabbatical so I could travel."

"That's fantastic. I love hearing stories of people taking the time out of their traditional (I used the air quotes gesture) lives to live their dreams. Good for you."

"Yeah, it's really great. I love my job but I was getting really burned out, you know? I really love my kids and I've been staying in touch with them, too."

"That's so great. I met another teacher on my trip also. She's an American and took a year sabbatical as well. Where do you plan to go?"

A Most Improbable Adventure

"I don't have it all figured out quite yet. I'm going to spend some time in South America and also in Australia; I have friends and family there."

"Have you been to other countries in your previous travels as well?"

"Yes, I've done loads of traveling before, but nothing like this. It makes me a bit nervous, actually."

"I bet you'll learn a lot along the way. You'll be uncomfortable a lot, and from that you'll learn about yourself."

"Have you done lots of traveling?"

"I've done some. My wife and I did a trip around the world a few years ago. I even wrote a book about it."

"Really? I'd love to read it."

"I hope you do."

"Where is your wife now?"

"She's back home in Canada with my two sons."

"How old are your sons?"

"Sam is three-and-a-half and Will is eight months."

"Wow! You have two very young boys and you're here in Central America traveling alone?

"I get that reaction a lot. Yes, my family is back home and I'm out exploring the world. I know, I know. My wife is really something special."

"I'd say. She must have her hands full."

"That she does. Her mom is helping out, too."

"Well, that's really quite amazing."

Just then my café mocha arrived at our table and I immediately took a sip. It was just the way I liked it; a coffee-chocolate balance that favours the coffee ever so slightly – just enough to make it interesting.

"Are you Heynor?" I asked the man who brought it to me.

"Si," he replied.

"I was told to tell you that Flaco sent me."

"Ah, yes, Flaco. He sends lots of people here."

"I assume he sends people here because the coffee is good?"

"Well, I guess you'll have to tell me if it's true."

"Well, just that one sip was excellent. I assume the rest will be equally good."

Donna and I went on to discuss our travel experiences from years past, including both good and challenging times. Just then I heard a man's voice from behind me.

"There you are."

I turned to see Stijn, Donna's friend, approaching.

"I wasn't sure if this was the right place," he said.

"Yeah, this is it," Donna replied.

"Hello," I said, as I extended my hand to shake his. "I'm Jason."

"I'm Stijn," he replied. "It's nice to meet you."

"The crazy Dutchman," Donna interjected.

"Yeah, that's right," he chuckled.

"Do you want to sit down?" she asked him.

"I thought maybe about getting something to eat. Did you want to find a place and grab a bite, maybe?

"Do you fancy supper?" Donna asked me.

"Yeah, sure, that's a great idea.

"Right then, let's finish our coffees and go," she said.

"Sounds good."

We walked the streets rather aimlessly for a few minutes and then settled on a place. As we sat down for dinner I got the feeling Stijn was burned out. He was on a three-week holiday in Costa Rica to try and relax but he seemed rather tense to me, or perhaps it was just his style. I hadn't known that many crazy Dutchmen, after all. His bespectacled face was tense around the eyes and his round face wore a look that dripped of disappointment.

"I came to Costa Rica for a holiday, to relax. It's been difficult. The travel has been difficult on me," he said dejectedly.

"Have you been sick on your trip," I asked.

"I've had some kind of cold."

"Maybe you'll feel better soon."

"I don't know. This trip hasn't been what I expected, you know?"

"How do you mean?"

"Well, the weather has been shit. I might as well have been in Amsterdam. It's been raining like crazy."

"It really was coming down in buckets yesterday," Donna offered. "It's been cold like England."

"Well, it is rainy season, and we are in a cloud forest," I said, half smiling.

"True," Donna replied, "but everything I had read said to expect short rains most days in the afternoon, not heavy rain all bloody day."

"Well, hopefully it clears up," I said, trying to lighten the mood. "I'd like to do a tour or a hike tomorrow. I plan to leave for San José the day after that. Would you guys be interested in a hike tomorrow?"

"I'd be into something," Donna replied. "How about you Stijn, fancy a hike in the forest?"

"If it's not raining I could do that," he replied, half-heartedly.

"Great, let's talk to Flaco when we get back and get signed up for something," I said, in as upbeat a way as I could muster without sounding annoyingly positive.

As it turned out I wasn't able to take the tour I wanted because, yet again, there were not enough people signed up for it. Instead we settled on going to the Monteverde Cloud Forest Biological Reserve. All we had to do was tell Flaco we wanted the 10:30am shuttle.

Our choice of departure time ultimately bit us in the ass because the rain started promptly an hour later. It was an enjoyable and easy hike to that point though the only things we saw in the forest were American college students working on a conservation project. No birds, no animals, no snakes.

The forest itself was a never-ending onslaught of green. Whenever I caught a glimpse of something that wasn't green it turned out to be the common dragon flower. The trunks of most trees were covered in green moss, any rare open spaces had green groundcover; it was inescapably green – hence the name of the reserve: Monteverde. It was a pleasant walk, however, not particularly hilly or difficult, on an excellent and well-used trail. The trail, however, turned into a rushing torrent as the rain pounded down on us in big, fat, drops.

Stijn was not having much fun. Donna had wet feet. I was just enjoying being outside. I particularly enjoyed the fact that I could breathe deeply and not inhale bus exhaust; smoke from steaming piles of trash; or the hot, humid stench of urine and feces. To me there was no better place to be than in the middle of a cloud forest – away from the cities and congestion, and mess.

"Stijn wants to go back to Holland early," Donna told me as we walked through the rain. "He's tired. He's going to see if he can change his flight."

"That's a long way to go to cut a trip short. Maybe if he had some warm weather he'd feel differently," I offered.

"Maybe, we'll see."

That night I barely slept. I tossed and turned and thought about nothing in particular. The alarm on my phone was due to ring at 5:30am but I hadn't slept since around 4:00am so I rolled out of bed and began to get ready. The bus wasn't leaving for another couple of hours but already I was dreading the bumpy ride back down the mountain.

Donna and Stijn decided they would join me as they were going back to warm weather in Puerto Viejo. They had to transfer to another bus in San José and spend another four hours in transit. Neither of them looked up to it at that time in the morning.

The taxi was actually on time, rather surprising all of us as we waited. The ride to the bus terminal in Santa Elena was a short one, taking only a few minutes. We got tickets and got ready to board. As I turned to my right near the ticket office I saw the German girl I had seen in Rivas, Nicaragua and then again at the Costa Rican border. I was hardly tired of seeing her as she was simply beautiful and she flashed a perfect white smile as she saw me. We chatted briefly about how strange it was that we had run into each other so often over the previous weeks. It turned out she and her boyfriend were going back to Germany from Panama City a week after me.

After paying two dollars to the driver for the privilege of putting my backpack into the dusty cargo hold of the bus I boarded and sat down. Donna sat beside me and Stijn across the aisle. He still didn't look very happy. He looked to me like he was ready to go home – a disappointed look in his eyes. I remembered that look – from Isabelle during our trip around the world. I remembered that feeling – I'd had it myself at times during that very same trip. Stijn's look said "I'm tired. I'm not enjoying this anymore. The travel is wearing me out and I'd rather be home, sitting on my comfortable couch and relaxing." I couldn't blame him. Sometimes things just don't go the way you expect them to. Sometimes it may be better to simply go home rather than force it. Of course, sometimes it's also better to actually push through it to get to the other side. In some ways my entire trip was about pushing through to the other side. Donna was trying to convince him of the wisdom of sticking with it but he seemed to have his mind made up. I resisted my temptation to get in the middle of it and just let them talk it out.

Upon arrival we partook in another unofficial taxi ride – the driver flashed us a useless plastic badge that hung around his neck; it had no picture of him, no text, no anything that would suggest it was official in any way. In fact it looked more like the back of a playing card than anything else. Donna couldn't help herself and inquired, multiple times in multiple ways, if he was, in fact, a real taxi driver. "It's okay, no problem," was his repeated reply. For only a couple of dollars I couldn't give a shit if he was just a random guy with a beat up old car or a trained driver that was part of a unionized fleet of shiny brand-new Cadillacs. After a few unnecessarily hard corners and rumbling over what I can only describe as urban ruins he dropped us in front of our hostel and then waited at the curb. We then decided to cross the street to another hostel after we learned that the room rate shown online was, in fact, a big old lie (this pissed off Stijn even more). The taxi driver continued to wait, for what I didn't know.

The room rate across the street was not much better but at least I didn't feel lied to. Stijn and Donna had stayed there on their way into Costa Rica a few weeks prior. I figured if they had stayed there before then it must be okay. I could not have been more wrong. Perhaps its only redeeming quality was a large yard with a modest pool, around which a dozen or so young travelers seemed to be enjoying themselves. It's only one night, I thought, so it didn't matter how awful it was. As long as the high razor-wire fences surrounding the property held up, and the multiple security cameras were working, everything would be just fine.

My room, on the other hand, left very much to be desired. The brown linoleum floor gave way to a yellow, pink, blue, brown, and red—possibly blood?—smattering of paint on the wall – cracked and peeling like sunburned skin. The bathroom consisted of a horribly mismatched toilet and sink, holes in the walls of various depths, crawling ants throughout, and a shower only slightly larger than a plane lavatory. I quickly placed it in the Top 10 Worst Rooms of my many travels. Then I saw the bed. I believe the sheet intended to be white, perhaps twenty years before, but its retched, tattered, multi-fluid stained existence on that particular day put that intention very much in doubt. Rather quickly the room – the dungeon, really – vaulted into the Top 5 Worst Rooms. I felt like draping a medal of achievement on the door handle alerting passers-by to this most high accomplishment, but, alas, there wasn't one on which to hang it.

Job number one after recovering from the shock of the room was to buy the bus ticket to Panama City for the following day. I didn't want to get stuck in the dungeon for any longer than absolutely necessary. I asked the young woman at the front desk for some assistance.

"Do you know if it's possible to buy a Tica Bus ticket over the phone," I inquired. I already knew the answer would be no but I wanted to test her to see exactly what I was dealing with.

"No, I don't think so. I think you need to go to the terminal to buy a ticket. Where do you want to go?" she replied.

"Panama City, tomorrow."

"Hmmmmm, tomorrow, I don't know," she said, wincing slightly, like she had just stubbed her toe.

"What do you mean you don't know?"

"I'm not sure. You should go to the terminal."

"Where is the terminal?" I asked patiently, yet with a hint of annoyance.

"I don't know."

"So you think I should go to the terminal but you don't know where it is?"

"No, I'm not sure."

I produced an old Tica Bus ticket from my pocket that showed the address—I knew I would need it again at some point—and gave it to her. "This is the address here," I pointed. "Do you know where it is?"

She looked at it very briefly and quickly said with confidence, "It's twelve blocks from here."

How could she not know where it is and then within two seconds of looking at the address know that it was exactly twelve blocks away? I started to get a little frustrated.

"Do you have a map showing where we are and where the terminal is?" I asked.

"No."

"No?"

"No."

"Okay, I guess I'll take a taxi then. Before I do that though, could you possibly call the terminal for me and ask if it's possible to get a ticket for tomorrow?"

She snatched the paper from my hand. She made the call, twice, but nobody answered.

"Sorry, nobody was there," she said.

"Okay, would you mind calling one of those other numbers? Those are the numbers for the agencies that work with Tica Bus. Thanks."

Again she snatched the paper from my hand. A deep exhale told me she was having about as much fun as I was. She dialed. No answer.

"Sorry, no answer."

"Well, thanks for trying. Could you please call me a taxi then? I'll just have to go there, I guess."

She quickly grabbed the phone, spoke incredibly fast, and slammed the phone back down. "It will be here in a minute."

"Muchas gracias."

"De nada."

In less than a minute I heard a horn honking outside. The taxi was there already.

"Tica Bus terminal, por favor," I said as I stepped in.

Without a response the taxi driver hit the gas and we were off. After driving for what seemed like hours we arrived at the terminal. The meter read just two dollars. In my painfully awkward Spanish I was able to convey that I wanted him to wait while I went inside and got my ticket. Amazingly he seemed to understand what I wanted and I dashed inside.

After finally finding the correct line I stood not moving ahead for quite some time. I tapped the shoulder of an older gentleman that stood directly in front of me.

"Perdón, Señor. Habla Ingles?"

"Yes," he replied.

"Can you tell me what's happening? We seem to be standing still here."

"The computer system is down. Nothing seems to be working."

"Oh, that sucks. Would you mind holding my spot in line here? I've got a taxi on the meter waiting for me outside."

A Most Improbable Adventure

"Sure, no problem."

I quickly ran out, paid the driver, and ran back in. I was gone about a minute. As I came back in the guy I asked to hold my spot was walking out.

"I've given up," he said as he approached me.

"Thanks for your fucking help," I said under my breath as I walked past him.

I suddenly found myself at the back of a Disneyland-sized lineup, waiting to buy a ticket on a system that wasn't working. Thankfully, amazingly, the system came back online and I was able to get my precious ticket – losing only about two hours in the process. With my ticket in hand I felt relieved and ready to head back to the hostel to relax. I stood in front of the terminal, expecting that I'd see taxis either lined up or arriving periodically. After several minutes it became apparent that I might be standing there until the following day unless I actively started looking for a taxi. I began to haphazardly walk the streets, heading, generally, in the direction I believed the hostel to be, seeking out the ubiquitous red taxi.

After a few random streets left me empty handed I headed toward what I thought would be the busier streets, assuming I'd spot a taxi there. Unfortunately, despite very heavy traffic in both directions, there were no taxis to be found. Had it been a few hours later in the day I may have been accused of attempted suicide as I had absolutely no business being where I was. A skinny white target would have stood out at night in a city known for its violent streets. Fortunately I had some time before darkness fell.

As I continued to scan the scene I spotted a red taxi about two blocks away. As I approached it I lobbed one of my lanky arms into the air and waved it like a schoolgirl at a boy band concert. I may have actually shouted out like a schoolgirl too, "Taxi! Taxi!" Unfortunately the taxi was already completely filled to the rim with people who no doubt knew where they were too and were extremely happy to be in its relative safety.

I felt a pang of jealousy as I saw the happy faces of two young couples in the next taxi that blew past me, nearly running me off the sidewalk in the process.

Finally, after wandering for a few hours, I spotted a taxi parked in front of a small shop – the kind of place that offered rice, beans, and some sort of dead animal for an extremely cheap price, as well as Coke, Fanta, and any number of cell phone brands. It was just sitting there, empty, with nobody nearby, or other sign of life. I walked toward it, my eyes darting from side to side hoping desperately that no one would jump out from behind a pile of trash and take it from me. I wasn't even worried about being mugged at that point – I was solely focused on getting a taxi and getting the hell out of wherever I was.

The taxi gods smiled upon me a moment later as a kind looking older gentleman exited the store and approached the driver's side of the car. "Taxi!" I yelled, rather exuberantly. I was only across a narrow street from him so I didn't need to be quite so loud. "Si," he replied. I was awash in relief as I fell into the back seat. I simply told him the name of the hostel, which he seemed to understand, and we were off.

Nobody in their right mind looks forward to a 16-hour bus ride. I guess I wasn't in my right mind, at least not completely. Though I dreaded the heaving and rocking and rattling and trying desperately to sleep in an uncomfortable seat with my legs jammed into the back of the seat in front of me I did look forward to finishing that last leg of the trip. I couldn't wait to again sleep in a real bed in a real hotel where I had a legitimate shot of making it from the bed to the bathroom without being taken down and slowly devoured by an incensed army of ants or other nasty creepy crawlers.

The next morning I said my goodbyes to Stijn and Donna, wishing them well. I knew Donna would struggle at first without him but would find her way as her travels continued. I hoped Stijn would find whatever he was looking for. Maybe

A Most Improbable Adventure

he really just had a cold and did not enjoy his vacation, maybe he was searching for something, I would never know.

I arrived early at the terminal despite the taxi taking a series of looping lefts and rights to rack up the fare. An extra dollar or two didn't mean much to me but it certainly did to him so I didn't say anything. All I wanted was to get to the terminal in one piece with enough time to check in. The unnecessary burning of an irreplaceable fossil fuel did not rank high on my list of concerns.

Mercifully, the seat beside me remained empty as the bus slowly pulled out of its barbed wire and steel cage enclosure and into the streets of San José. I overheard a couple of guys speaking English a few rows ahead of me; otherwise I seemed to be the lone tourist. I settled in for the arduous journey trying to think only of being in a comfortable bed and then being in my own bed a few days later. I pulled out my cell phone and touched the camera icon. Until San José was left behind I watched short videos on my phone of my two wonderful sons, tears welling up in my eyes. I missed them horribly and could not wait to hold them in my arms again. Things changed quickly at their young ages, especially Will, who was just a baby. I could almost feel him in my arms and smell that unmistakable baby smell as I kissed him on the head. It was time to go home.

I nodded off into a sloppy sleep a couple of times during the first half of the trip. We stopped only once for a break – at a purpose-made restaurant serving the traditional rice and beans I had grown to despise. I chose to eat a few cookies instead. With surprising swiftness we had reached the border and thus I filed out to let the good people in the Costa Rica Immigration department know that I was leaving.

In front of me in line stood the two guys I had overheard earlier speaking English. One of them, a fresh-faced young man, spoke with a heavy German accent. The other one, Alex, sounded just like me, and it turned out he was from

Mississauga, one of the many cities that make up the mess that is the Greater Toronto Area where I lived.

"Have you been traveling long?" I inquired.

"A couple of months in Central America, but I've been living in Vietnam for the past nine years," he replied.

"Really? Nine years. Doing what?"

"I'm a teacher. I've been teaching English."

"Do you ever plan to go back to Canada?"

"Well, I told myself I'd make that decision by the time I turned forty. I'm only thirty-seven now so I have a few years still."

"That sounds like a plan."

"Yeah, my parents have been wondering when I'm going to come back. I'll be there at Christmas this year. I haven't seen snow in nearly a decade so it's going to be hard."

He was extremely tanned for a fair-haired, blue-eyed Canadian so going back to winter was probably the last thing he wanted. He had acclimated to the heat and humidity of Southeast Asia obviously, as he looked very comfortable in the evening heat while I dripped with sweat.

After another conversation-free exchange with yet another lifeless immigration officer I hurried to catch up to my countryman and the German, largely because I had no idea where the hell to go – signage was not prevalent in Central America after all. All three of us walked, aimlessly, hoping someone would speak up and tell us where to go next. It wasn't clear if we were still in Costa Rica or if we had entered Panama. We just kept walking until we stumbled upon an official-looking, though seriously run down, building.

"Ah, there we go," I said, as I spotted a sign that read Salida (Exit). "That must be where we go. I guess we haven't left quite yet."

A large, dark, middle-aged man with a badge hanging around his neck fired a few words at me in rapid Spanish. He saw the befuddled look on my face and repeated, "One dollar to exit." I rummaged around in my pocket for a one dollar bill and handed it to him. In exchange he put some sort of sticker in my passport.

Once I had passed all the tests and answered all the silly questions it was time to engage in the other time-waster: the baggage check. Everyone gathered their bags and entered a tiny little room that surely was used to interrogate and assault the bad guys. The room barely contained us all and had only two tables and a chair in it. I noticed that some people had already put their bags on the tables and began to unzip them so I did the same. We then waited for a half-hour while various official-looking people wandered in and out, not looking at us nor talking to anyone.

Then a stocky man with a large gun at his side entered the room. He spoke for a few seconds and then promptly left. Nobody moved. A few minutes later another official entered the room and sat down on the lone chair. He began reading names on a list he held on a clipboard. I assumed it was a roll call to check bags, as opposed to a list of people about to be shot. The first few names elicited a simple "Aquí," "Presente," or "Si." These people were then ushered off into an even smaller room to the side – one I didn't even see when I first came in. A few minutes passed while the roll call continued until we were all accounted for.

The gruelling bag inspection took some time as the half-asleep officials went through the motions, pretending to be gravely concerned over the contents of our bags. They tended to spend the most time reviewing people's underwear and selection of magazines. A brief debate broke out with one young traveler who did not want to break the tiny lock on his backpack, given he had somehow misplaced the key. That didn't stop the inspector from pulling out a handy tool that cut through it with ease. My bag received the typical cursory glance that it had been getting the entire trip. I looked like a harmless dad, after all.

Back on the bus where I had left my small backpack nearly two hours before, Alex and I debated the merits of such border crossings and decided, rather than focussing on them as a bit of a farce, to let it be and just be happy to be moving on. I settled in for a few more hours of uncomfortable tossing and turning. Fourteen hours after departure, and, amazingly, two hours *ahead* of schedule, we arrived in Panama City, the final leg of my most improbable adventure.

LEAVING AMERICA

Unlike the so-called bus terminals in other Central American countries, which were often nothing more than a patch of dirt (or rubble and trash) with a bench (sometimes) nearby, the Panama City bus terminal was a palace. It looked more like an airport terminal; high ceilings, bank machines, bathrooms (for a fee, of course), and wide staircases. It was open, airy and it felt odd to see after all that had preceded it. It was a welcome sight after such a long trip.

There were only a handful of taxis sitting outside; it was 3:00am after all. I struggled mightily to communicate with an extremely overweight and rather angry looking taxi driver as to where I wanted to go. He looked at me like I had asked him to take me to Mars. He shook his head as if to say he had never, ever, heard of such a hotel or the street it was on. He was so vigorous in his belief that I actually second-guessed myself for a moment, wondering if I had the wrong name and street, perhaps from another of the stops on my trip—fourteen hours of bus travel can do that to a person. Having come to terms with the fact that I was, in fact, correct, and sane, I pressed on with my request. Again, he looked stunned, deeply concerned about my request and mumbled something I interpreted to mean maybe he did, in fact, know what I was talking about. He was messing with me of course—something I would come to realize soon enough.

"Cuánto cuesta?" I asked.

Again he mumbled something – it wasn't Spanish and it sure as hell was not English. It was a straight-up mumble.

"Cuánto cuesta?" I repeated.

Again with the mumbling. I thought I heard him say "Cinco" or something similar. My guidebook said it would be three, maybe four, dollars for a taxi to the hotel but at 3:00am I could care less if it was five. I wanted to rest my weary head on a nice, fluffy pillow, and was not about to argue over a dollar. I agreed, and we were off.

Exactly six minutes later we had arrived. I thought it was pretty fast for a guy who seemed so deeply confused about the existence of such a hotel. Clearly he was playing games with me. He parked the car, turned his fat head toward me in the back seat and said "Veinte."

"Veinte?" I repeated, my voice crackling with surprise. The anger was starting to creep in.

"Si, veinte," he said as he pointed to the small clock on the dashboard. I assumed that he meant there was some kind of premium based on the time of day.

"No veinte," I exclaimed.

"Si veinte," he repeated.

Then I lost it and blasted him. "There is no fucking way I am paying you twenty dollars for a six-minute ride!"

"Si, veinte," he said, gesticulating toward the tiny dashboard clock again.

"Seis minutos! Seis minutos! No veinte dólares para seis minutos!" I yelled.

"Si, veinte, veinte!"

I was tired, aggravated, and not in the mood to get into it with that particular mass of humanity so I offered a compromise. "Diez. Diez solamente."

"No. No. Veinte," he said again, pointing to the clock on the dashboard.

A Most Improbable Adventure

"Uno momento," I said, holding my finger in the air, indicating I needed a moment to do something. I opened the car door, jumped out, and went up the stairs to the entrance of the hotel. I knocked on the glass, jarring awake a young man who was sleeping on a couch nearby. He jumped up and began unlocking the door.

I poked my head inside. "Habla Ingles?"

"No," he replied.

"Shit," I said out loud. I lingered there for a moment, selling the idea to the taxi driver that I was getting advice suggesting he was trying to rob me by charging me twenty bucks. I returned to the car, unloaded my bags and dropped them on the sidewalk. I reached into my pocket, grabbed a ten dollar bill and leaned into the car with one knee on the back seat.

"Diez es bueno," I said, forcefully thrusting my clenched hand with the cash toward his fat face. In a flash he snatched it. I didn't wait for a verbal response; I just got out of the car and slammed the door, hard. As I walked up the steps to the hotel I glanced back to see if he was going to get out and come after me. He sat in his seat, crumpled the bill and put it in his pocket. He didn't look pleased, but he didn't look angry either, he simply put the car into drive and stepped on the gas.

Relieved, I dragged my tired ass up the stairs to the entrance. By that time the young man had found, or awoken, someone who looked like they might know what the heck to do. The young woman spoke only broken English so it was a challenge to get any real confirmation as to what was going on. I wasn't supposed to check in until twelve hours later so technically she could have made me wait that length of time, possibly lying flat on the marble floor where I stood – not entirely a bad option given how ragged and tired I was.

"*Ees* okay to check now," she said.

"Now?" I said, surprised to the point of nearly crying with happiness at my incredible luck.

"Si, yes, now," she replied, not looking particularly happy about it. It was the middle of the night after all.

"Muchas gracias! I gushed. Then I thought to myself – am I going to be charged for an extra day? It's one thing to check in early; it's entirely another to check in early and not pay anything more.

"Is my rate still the same?" I asked.

"Que?" she replied.

"It won't cost me anything more, yes?

"It still same," she said, though looking a little unsure of herself.

"Okay, so I can check in early and still pay what my reservation says," I said, showing her the crumpled piece of paper I had printed off when I made my reservation.

"Si. Same."

When I opened the door to my room I couldn't believe what I saw. It was a clean, modern room, with white sheets and a large-screen TV on the wall. It was in stark contrast to what I had experienced to that point on my journey. There were no questionable stains on the wall and bed covers, no scurrying insects on the floor, no decrepit furniture and peeling paint, and no horrific odour. I looked into the bathroom and felt as though I had just walked into a high-end spa: sparkling clean, it smelled of lavender and had crisp, clean towels hanging on the rack. The shower door was spotless; the toilet was modern and lacked both the stains and stench I had come to expect. It was oddly unsettling to be looking at a clean and modern room after having become so used to squalor.

After coming to realize that I was, indeed, awake and not dreaming I stripped down and stepped into the shower. Forgetting where I was my body recoiled at the feeling of truly hot water on my skin. It was a real luxury and it felt so good I could have stood there for days just letting it melt me and wash me away down the drain.

I eased into the cushy soft bed and let it swallow me up. I slept like a baby until mid-morning. When I awoke I went to the dining area—a real let-down given the quality of the room—and struggled to put down a meagre buffet breakfast. After which I made arrangements for a city tour for the following day.

I walked the streets of Panama City for a few hours, proving to myself that I could actually find my present location on a map I had ripped out of a tourist magazine. I wasn't inspired to see much, I just wanted to walk the streets and take it in. It was different than the rest of Central America in one significant way – there were skyscrapers at every turn. When my eyes were raised up I felt like I could have been in any North American city. When my eyes fell back down I saw garbage-strewn streets, crumbling low-rise buildings, and wildly coloured chicken buses blowing thick black smoke into the air as they tore down the road.

Vehicles went flying past as I waked along Avenida Balboa. Every second car seemed to be an SUV – whether a Mercedes, Audi, Toyota, BMW, or Lexus. Unlike nearly everywhere else I had been in Central America the city seemed to have the kind of wealth that was either unseen or non-existent elsewhere. As I walked my view always included a skyscraper in some state of construction; cranes littered the sky as they did in Toronto and many other big cities around the world.

Stepping out of the heat for a brief reprieve I entered one of the city's many shopping malls. I felt a bit peckish so I headed for the food court. Scanning the bustling scene I saw the sign for Subway and suddenly I felt the need for a sandwich. The line was short so I headed there.

Even though there were only four people in front of me it took thirty-five minutes to get a six-inch Subway Club. As I waited in line I overheard two people behind me speaking English, though with Indian accents. I made eye contact with one of them and said, "It sure is taking a while, isn't it?"

"Oh, my goodness, yes. This is unbelievable. There's only one person doing anything back there," one of them replied.

"Where are you gentlemen from?" I asked.

"We're from the U.S." replied the one wearing a quintessential Panamanian hat. "You would never get service like this in the U.S." he continued, somewhat disgusted.

"Are you traveling in Panama?" I asked.

"Yes, we've spent three weeks in Central America and we're heading home tomorrow."

"Oh, I've spent five weeks in Central America and I head home the day after tomorrow," I replied, chuckling.

We continued our dialogue as we waited for the slow-moving, disinterested, Subway employees to deliver our elusive sandwiches. We agreed to sit down together to chat a bit more.

We were joined by their wives, who were patiently waiting as well. I was introduced to them all – A.J. in the hat, Jagdish (Jack) and their wives whose names I forgot the moment they were uttered. They were from Las Vegas and had lived there for over thirty years. A.J. and Jack were retired engineers. Jack was an author, having published three books, one in English called *The Seven Cs of Happiness*. They were pleased to know that I had spent five weeks in India during my world trip several years before.

"India is so crowded, and so dirty," Jack blurted out.

"Oh, so dirty," his wife followed up.

"We are so glad to not be living there. We are used to the United States and we like it there. There are different challenges in the States, but cleanliness is not a problem," she continued.

"I had some interesting experiences there, to be sure," I said.

"What did you like best?" A.J. inquired.

"You know, I get that question a lot, I mean *a lot*. Over the years I have been unable to really put my finger on exactly what it is I liked the best. You've probably heard it before – India tends to be a love-hate thing with most Westerners. Such amazing beauty and history and yet so frustrating!"

"I have heard that many times," Jack replied. "When we go back it's the same thing. We are basically Westerners now, after thirty years, and we find it very frustrating too."

"One thing I really appreciated about the experience was being able to drop my typical Western attitudes and approaches and act more, well, Indian. By that I mean that I spent some time simply trying to fit in, rather that fighting against the tide of a billion people and thousands of years of culture. It was extremely liberating – uncomfortable but liberating."

"It's not easy to do, is it?" asked Jack.

"No, but when you do, rather when I did, it was quite a feeling. I just went after what I wanted and did it in the context of the moment, not trying to be too Canadian – you know, reserved and quiet. I went the other way – just going with the flow. It worked out well – I got what I wanted and didn't seem to upset anyone."

"It sounds like you had an interesting time there," Jack said.

"I did indeed. The whole trip was amazing. This trip has been awesome, too. I never would have thought that I would have met the people that I have, including four Indians, living in the U.S. and having lunch at a mall in Panama City!"

"That's the great thing about traveling, isn't it?" A.J. commented.

"That's for sure," I said. We continued to chat briefly and quietly ate our sandwiches before parting and heading our separate ways.

The next day I went to see one of my bucket list items – the Panama Canal. In a bus full of a dozen tourists I was the only English-speaking visitor. The guide was bilingual so I felt like I got my own one-on-one tour. The canal itself is not much to look at – a set of locks that could be found in most any other country in the world that requires navigation between two bodies of water at different elevations. For me it was more about the magnitude of the accomplishment, especially given the technology at the time, and the impact to the world as a result.

The Panama Canal project, which connected the Atlantic and Pacific Oceans for the first time, was undertaken by the French in 1881, when Panama was a province of Colombia, but was then taken over by the United States in 1904 (not surprisingly, the U.S. helped Panama separate from Colombia in 1903). They completed the project in August of 1914. Ships no longer had to traverse the dangerous Cape Horn at the southern tip of South America and could now quickly pass through the isthmus from one side to the other in a day or so. This effectively brought the west coast of North and South America into the world economy in a much more integrated way.

The U.S. maintained control over the Canal Zone until 1977 when control was then shared with Panama. Official control was passed to Panama in 1999 and the zone is now managed by the Panama Canal Authority, a Panamanian government agency. As I stood there watching a massive boat, carrying what must have been thousands of containers, pass through the locks I thought about how long it would have otherwise taken to get around the entire South American continent to deliver those containers. In today's world we think largely of technological gadgets as game changers, but what a game changer the canal must have been nearly a hundred years ago.

The next day I found myself at the Panama City airport; my journey had come to an end. Where had the time gone? Was I really ready to go home? As I stood in line for my next-to-last security check I met John, a man originally from New York who lived in Panama City.

"This is a great country. The States is so messed up right now. I see no reason to be there. I've got everything I could ask for here in Panama."

"When did you move here?" I asked.

A Most Improbable Adventure

"2004. I hope to become a citizen at some point," he replied.

"Wow, really? You are giving up your citizenship?"

"Oh yeah, absolutely. This place is so much more relaxed yet has everything you could need. Things are so messed up in the U.S."

"I'd agree with that," a voice came from over my shoulder. A tall, thin, white-bearded man, likely in his seventies, was in the security line as well and decided to offer his opinion.

"Are you an American also?" I asked.

"Yes, though I was born here, in the early forties in the Canal Zone. My parents were in the military," he replied.

"You don't want to live in the U.S. either?" I inquired.

"No. I like to travel there once in a while but I prefer to live here."

"Interesting," I said. "Maybe you are both on to something."

It was then my turn to head through the security check so I scurried along, turning back to give them both a nod. "Good luck gentlemen," I offered, and moved on.

I walked away fascinated by the fact that Americans, at least a few of them anyway, didn't want to live in America. Was it really *that* bad? Were these the outliers? I thought back to Lindsay, who I had met in Nicaragua and who lived in Costa Rica. She had no real desire to return home to New York either. She, too, thought things in the U.S. had gone off the rails and she didn't see any great benefit to living there. Colin, in León, and Caitlan, in Granada, both chose to live in Nicaragua rather than the U.S. I had gathered a small sample size, to be sure, but the sentiment seemed to be that *Central* America was a better place to be than the *United States of* America. Perhaps they were simply seeking fulfillment just as I was – and had found it, or were on the path to it, in new places.

On the flight home I thought about possibilities. One of the many things I love about unstructured travel adventures is that I take away great memories not just of the big bucket list items but of the things that surprised me along the way. I take detours, side-trips, and see completely unplanned sights. I end up seeing volcanic explosions up close. I meet people I would have never met otherwise and hear some truly amazing stories. It seems the more improbable my adventure is someone else is having an even more improbable one—and we get to be part of each other's stories.

Is it possible for an unemployed man in his forties, married and a father of two young children, to travel through several countries not likely on the bucket lists of most people—some considered dangerous—and come out alive and more fulfilled on the other side? The fact that I did it and am writing this now would suggest that the answer is yes. It was at a very challenging time in my life that I decided to take this particular adventure and I came back not just alive but more alive.

Much of the rich value in life can only be found on the fringes – at the edges of your mind and at the edges of your comfort zone. To live fully requires that you go there and see what you might find. I had gone to the edge, in many ways, *simply by going* to Central America. I met some amazing people that had gone to the edge too. Looking into their eyes I could see that they had touched a place within themselves that had deep meaning for them. They had all navigated their very different lives and had reached a degree of fulfillment by traveling and pushing their limits.

Life, they say, is short. I have come to realize that this is not necessarily true. I believe that a *fulfilled* life can be short. It's possible to live to be a hundred years old – but how fulfilling will those years be? Earl lived a relatively short life, but it was fulfilled. His passing was a reminder that I needed to focus on that fulfillment and take action that would lead me in that direction. Living long was not necessarily my goal; living fully was. The opportunity presented to me was one I could not pass up so I took it. I met with constant reminders along the way of what is important and I am changed as a result; how could I not be?

I developed an even greater appreciation for my wife on this adventure. Many strangers I spoke to about her thought I was blessed to have someone like her in my life. They recognized, and reinforced, what I already knew – that Isabelle is a gift in my life. She knows me better than I know myself sometimes. She sees in me what I am sometimes blind to – consciously or unconsciously. Her idea, and love for me, enabled me to experience this most improbable adventure. She had many choices for how to react to my situation. She could have literally chosen any course of thinking, and action. What did she think about? She thought about me.

Being separated from my boys was at times very difficult. There were occasions, however, where I appreciated being able to sleep the whole night through, which I hadn't done in the nearly eight months leading up to the trip. In exchange for some of those more restful nights I also got the displeasure of bouncing and shaking on overnight bus trips – the kind of punishment I would not wish on my worst enemies. The night I threw up on the bus I would have loved to hear Will's cry. Even though Will had not spoken a word, nor walked a step, nor asked for the keys to the car just yet, he was changing, and I was missing it. Seeing him and Sam on Skype warmed my heart, and broke it at the same time. Seeing Sam's smiling face and hearing his excited voice as he saw me tugged at my soul and made me wish I could reach right through the computer screen for a world-famous squeezy hug. Being away from them made me appreciate them even more and made me realize how much I craved their physical presence. I rue the day when they are too old to want to hug their daddy.

I thought about my brother Colin. The few days I spent with him after Earl's passing was perhaps the most important time we had spent together in our lives. Listening to Colin talk about Earl helped me gain insights into my brother, his thinking, and his life. I felt him with me during my times of anxiety and challenge on the trip. I knew he was watching over me, as he has his entire life. When I thought of him in this way I thought of an image I pull from my memory bank periodically – a picture of me as a baby, curled up in his then six-year-old arms on the chair in the living room of my grandparents' house. He's smiling for the camera but his eyes tell you he's thinking about something other than being cute for the picture. He has a look of realization that he has become a protector of the little bundle of joy in his arms. He knows he will somehow be responsible for this person; a burden that would take me many years to fully understand. Yes, he looks like he's six-years-old but somehow he also looks like a grown man. It's one of my favourite images of him. I can't put into words what it means to be able to pull that image whenever I want. It has gotten me through some difficult times in my life and it comforted me during the rough parts of this trip. I was able to connect with him from thousands of kilometres away.

Sometimes we don't realize how impactful someone has been in our life until they are no longer with us. I realized, during my time with Colin, that Earl had influenced Colin's life in more and deeper ways than I had ever even considered. Earl had therefore influenced me and my life without me even knowing it. Even before I was born Earl and Colin were best friends. My *entire* life had been influenced in some way by this man; someone who was taken from his earthly existence entirely too soon. During the trip I thought of Earl often. I thought about what he represented to Colin and how his life had impacted me. I thought about the gaping hole his leaving had left in Colin's life. I thought about how his passing had strongly influenced me to go on this adventure and live my life more fully. I still have a hard time believing he is actually gone.

It's so easy in life to forget to slow down and *feel* life. We get so wound up in our daily lives that we don't take the time to truly experience what is going on around us. That was my life before this particular adventure. As much as I thought I was living a full life I can see now that I really wasn't. All the requisite pieces were there, but the puzzle was not complete and the image was left undone. The picture started to become clearer simply by taking the risk and going to Central America under the circumstances that I did. I have since come to realize that the picture may never actually be complete – and that's okay. It's the pursuit of it that's important.

A key missing ingredient for me in this pursuit was not just fulfillment but gratitude. I'm so lucky to have the life I do. Having gone through this experience, as challenging as it was at times, I came out on the other side being grateful for it all. Even when I bitched about things underneath it all I was connecting with a sense of gratitude for even having had the chance to experience it.

I know anything is possible. I have lived possibilities. I have been changed by something that by all accounts I should not have even attempted. Should I go out and do something equally as improbable the next time the universe presents an opportunity masquerading as a challenge? It's been said that our lives are defined by the sum of the decisions that we make. I know the answer already.

Made in the USA
San Bernardino, CA
22 November 2016